The Roles of Organisation Development

Dr Garden brings her extensive consulting experience and in-depth knowledge of the field to identify key roles in organisational development. Her book is a brilliant guide to making change happen and uses self-assessments, exercises and a wide range of practical references. It is truly inspirational and an essential read for all leaders.

> *Ralph Lewis, Programme Director, London Business School, UK*

Annamaria Garden, a gifted OD consultant, dissects for us seven roles that are involved in this endeavor. With examples from her practice as well as her research, Dr Garden walks us through the different roles and the contexts to which they best apply. Her emphasis in each is on the psychological reality behind the organizational issues she confronts. She brings to her analysis a keen moral compass and invites us to follow her, whether we are consultants, managers, or just human beings. An intriguing book full of keen psychological insights.

> *Lotte Bailyn, Sloan School of Management, USA*

This book is dedicated in memory of my mother

The Roles of Organisation Development

ANNAMARIA GARDEN

Routledge
Taylor & Francis Group

LONDON AND NEW YORK

First published 2015 by Gower Publishing

2 Park Square, Milton Park, Abingdon, Oxon, OX14 4RN
605 Third Avenue, New York, NY 10017

Routledge is an imprint of the Taylor & Francis Group, an informa business

First issued in paperback 2020

British Library Cataloguing in Publication Data
A catalogue record for this book is available from the British Library.

Library of Congress Cataloging-in-Publication Data
Garden, Anna-Maria.
  The roles of organisation development / by Annamaria Garden.
    pages cm
  Includes bibliographical references and index.
  ISBN 978-1-4724-5414-0 (hardback)
  1. Organizational change. 2. Psychology, Industrial. 3. Organizational behavior. I. Title.
  HD58.8.G368 2015
  658.4'06--dc23

                                                              2015003944

ISBN 978-1-4724-5414-0 (hbk)
ISBN 978-0-367-73796-2 (pbk)

CONTENTS

LIST OF FIGURES

LIST OF TABLES

FOREWORD

The craft and practice of organization development has been with us now for well over 50 years and we are still evolving it. This book gives us a little history and very generously identifies some of us as having influenced the field. Annamaria Garden represents the next generation, one of our really good students, who got the message that the practice of OD is still evolving and there is lots of room for people like her to contribute something entirely new to our thinking about it.

Many books and articles have been written attempting to define the activities of organization development practitioners precisely, but mostly they have just added to the conceptual confusion while adding a multitude of "tools" for the improvement of a multitude of organizational tasks.

So why yet another book? Because this book takes a different tack toward telling us what organization development is and how to think about ourselves when we are working with an organization. This book tells us what roles those of us who engage in this practice can assume, what frameworks we can adopt in thinking about what we are doing, what insights we can gain from a more precise analysis of what kind of help we might provide.

As I contemplated these various roles I appreciated the fact that they are archetypal roles for thinking about any relationship. I have written about "helping" in general and found myself productively analyzing my own helping behavior whether as a friend, counselor, parent, or boss. This book brings us down from the abstractions that we academics are so fond of to ordinary language and ordinary concepts for thinking about how we relate to each other in a helping relationship, or, for that matter, in any relationship.

Reading about these roles and thinking about when and how I play them was not only fun but also very illuminating. You will enjoy reading this book and learn from it. I did.

Edgar H. Schein
Professor Emeritus
MIT Sloan School of Management

INTRODUCTION

I was once hired to teach the managers of a company which had just bought out Nokia. The message I had to give them was that they, in the newly acquiring company were, for the most part, to 'not go near Nokia'. Specifically, to not over-manage them. Why hire me to teach them that? They were already primed to think very carefully about how they manage this acquisition because they had woefully managed a prior acquisition in the US. They winced at what had happened in this latter company. However, they had, at least, been 'unfrozen'. My task was to teach them a case on this difficult acquisition and then begin a discussion on their new one, Nokia.

The primary reason they wanted this was that there was still an enormous danger of mismanagement because Nokia was small and they were large; they needed a massive cultural shift to do it and they had never achieved that before. Nokia was creative still and the acquiring company wanted to keep it that way. They, used to being a large action-oriented company, needed hearts and minds to be retrained for this new acquisition to be a success. Also, they had to assess the hearts and minds of Nokia for the acquisition to be a success. Action-man managers that they were, they needed to *sit still and wonder* for a while before doing anything to the new company. They knew that even one wrong sentence could harm the buy-out because of the sensitivities of the smaller Nokia. Each one of the top 200 managers in the larger acquiring company came through the workshop I ran with two others. My session could have been entitled 'Leaving Nokia to stand on its own two feet'/ or 'Not stepping on Nokia'.

The point was that these managers had to think and act more *psychologically* and wisely than they were used to. They were used to being micro-managers and, at that stage, were not very creative. What resources could they draw on? Is there a role they could draw on? Yes, I call it the Cultivator (Chapter 4). This role is where it makes best sense to train yourself to sit on your hands and wait. Is this what we learn in working with companies? No, – even OD people can become a bit like heroic managers.

As it happened, they were astute enough, particularly with a past failed acquisition as a contrast spurring them on, to be what I would call psychological interpreters/OD people, not just straightforward business managers. Many people would attribute the managers' actions to common sense. I view these actions from a psychological reference. They were being psychologically intelligent.

In this book I describe the roles OD people play (as well as managers) when they are being psychologically intelligent. To me, a psychological interpreter is a form of OD. The definition of OD by Dick Beckhard, a teacher of mine at MIT (Boston) and one of the founding fathers of OD, is as follows: " Organizational development is a planned systemwide change programme, using behavioral science knowledge to move the organization to a new state" (Beckhard, 1997, p. 76). My reference point in terms of "behavioural science" knowledge is primarily psychological. That is my particular bias.

I have never met an OD consultant who could, off the cuff, answer the question: "what do you do as an OD consultant"? Indeed this book sprang from a desire to answer a question posed to me by a consultant I was training up: "How do you do what you do?" she asked me. I didn't have a clue how to answer her question at first. Not until I had sat down years later to write about it. This book, and my previous book (Garden, 2000) are my answers to her question.

I have written this book thinking of three audiences: the professional OD or HR person, the student of management or OD, and the manager, who must make sense of the organisation they work in.

Breaking things into roles makes it easier to comprehend the gamut of what OD is about. Needless to say, these roles are also played by good managers. OD people tend to play these roles as a matter of course. However, they are to a large extent in practice implicit and not explicit. As Warner Burke states: "OD is more of a process than a step-by-step procedure" (Burke, 1994, p. 1). That is why it is hard to describe what you do as an OD person.

Some of what I describe as roles are different to the conventional roles ascribed to OD people. In particular, I emphasise the activity of bringing in 'content' not just 'process'. I think I make allowances for more 'content-based advice' than does the doyen of process consulting Professor Edgar Schein, who was another teacher of mine at MIT and one of the founding fathers of the OD field.

I hope my version is understood even by those who are OD people but have another way of trying to achieve the same aim: "I want to influence organizations to function in a more humane as well as high performing mode"" as Dick put it (Beckhard, 1997, p. xii).

CHAPTER 1

AN OD APPROACH

THE SEMINAR

Many years ago, when I was doing my PhD, I attended a seminar overseen, and attended by, Professor Ed Schein, the father of process consulting, and Professor Dick Beckhard, both founding fathers of OD and both my teachers. I was half aware of their significance and the other half of me rather blasé.

To Ed, this seminar was, apart from other things, part of the PhD's training in qualitative methods. The process that was devised was to have one person in the group act as a person in an organisation and they would be interviewed by the interviewer, also a member of the group. Ed's intention was to get us to see the idea of being client-centred. This meant pulling not pushing data out of the person (my words). The reason for doing it this way, according to Ed, was to get at the truth. If the person was pushed, you would not get at the truth but simply a compliant or defensive approach. This was Ed's key principle as far as I could see. To Dick, who was more interventionist, it was much more a process of making things happen. To him, he wanted also to get out the truth, which could occur by making things happen. The fundamental principle of both was to get the best situation, and information, to emerge. But their basic approaches were very different. As a novice to OD, I was riveted by this exchange. All I could figure out was that they were both right, and I thought that that probably wasn't what I was supposed to figure out. (Ed Schein wrote his version of this fascinating seminar in Schein, 1987)

Observing the Two Masters

What mattered most to we PhD students was only partly to discover the best principle for a client centred approach, but more to observe the two masters at work together. (I think Ed and Dick would not have been very amused if they knew what trivia we PhD students involved ourselves with). We would have long discussions about whether or not they were competing. Watching the seminar unfold week by week, and participating in the discussions that occurred outside this forum had to partly be our way of getting back at the powers that be that inflicted the torture of the PhD process on us.

There were moments when no one spoke. Trying to get the two 'schools' to agree was the obvious thing and most of us decided to live with the 'conflict', although there was long discussion about whether or not there was any conflict or whether they should agree. Sanity emerged on the day Professor Lotte Bailyn, herself a faculty member in the Organisational Studies Department, decided to be in the interviewee seat and Ed took up the role of interviewer. Lotte was interested in the whole process of interviewing so she could simply use this process designed by Ed, as a learning experiment. We proceeded on the next week with more guinea pigs.

WHICH MASTER TO FOLLOW

It was possible to learn more from this active approach to teaching than any formal course. I have often asked myself in the years that followed this event whether I practiced OD more in a way like Ed, or like Dick. Never have I been able to answer this question. What I do is a mix of the two approaches. In addition, what I have invented of my own is several things.

HAVING A PSYCHOLOGICAL BENT

The main one is that I have quite a psychological bent. This wasn't drummed into me when I was at MIT although my dissertation drew heavily from Carl Jung on my own initiative and there I used the Myers Briggs Type Indicator™ (MBTI™), supervised by Ed Schein. (There are several sections on Jung and the MBTI™ in the book). Once I had my PhD I went to London Business School on the research faculty, with a one day-a week consulting practice. At LBS I was called by my boss 'the culture person', integrating the Business Policy Department, where I sat along with the likes of Gary Hamel, John Stopford as well as a visiting Charles Hampden-Turner and an Emeritus Charles Handy, alongside an Organisational Behaviour Department with John Hunt, Rob Goffee and Gareth Jones. I left after five years to pursue my own OD consulting practice in London mainly because I could be more creative in the latter than at LBS. I definitely focused on culture (change usually) as well as pursuing such contracts as helping a company implement strategy faster, and various other OD work.

Psychology as an OD Tool

Why should psychology be so important? From OD's earliest beginnings, one key task has been that of recognizing when business decisions are being driven as much by the psychological factors present as they are by the business needs present. Traditionally, we think of this work as one involving process skills.

We've all seen conversations about business topics that actually are simply the vehicle through which psychological questions are addressed. In such situations, the reality is that people are sizing each other up, getting a picture of how everyone intends to play it, or figuring out who can count on whom. Similarly, time may be taken to discuss the details of a new decision, not because the decision is important but because, at base, the people involved are using it to get psychological answers in an indirect way.

VISIBLE AND INVISIBLE REALITIES

In organisations, the legitimacy of applying a financial or strategic framework to business does not need to be established. These approaches are well-established, clear doorways to reality. However, the same cannot be said for the psychological perspective. Here, in this unfamiliar territory one does need to establish legitimacy. This psychological perspective, as a separate framework through which you can discern events, is very unusual.

In OD, psychological work is more basic in its acceptance. I have referred to Dick Beckhard's formulation of OD before: he states that "OD is based on behavioural science knowledge" (Beckhard, 1969 p. 25). Note that Ed Schein emphasises, in Process Consultation Revisited the need to "understand the sociological dynamics of the helping relationship" (p. xii). Having a discipline as a base in OD work is a prerequisite. In the book I refer to several psychological sources, such as, Gestalt, Will Schutz, Jung, Assagioli and so on.

The theory I use most as a consultant is that of Carl Jung. I use his theory of the dynamics of the psyche rather than, for example, just his theory of psychological types, which informed the Myers Briggs Type Indicator™. When I lived in London I did a lot of workshops on the dynamics of the psyche as well – many weekends were spent with The Centre for Transpersonal Psychology and so on (See Chapter 8). I learnt quite a bit from all these workshops, seminars and practical homework. One thing was the thrust in the psyche to goodness. These were not shows to ferret out what is wrong in people's psyche, which is what I had learned about psychology as an undergraduate at University, but how people yearned for wholeness and health. A lot of my assumptions about working for organisations come from these same assumptions.

The psychological reality I'm speaking of is not the same thing as giving a high priority to human resources or valuing people as an 'asset'. The idea of the psychological perspective as a valid way of seeing organisational reality is different.

In talking about it, I'm concerned with more than understanding people's feelings or the inner needs of a leader. To truly talk about a psychological perspective is to go beyond understanding cerebral processes, such as logic and intuition. It is to go beyond seeing just emotional events, such as conflict and competition. It is to place psychological reality at the centre of the business; at the forefront. (See my previous article on psychological reality in organisations; Garden, 1998).

In my OD work, clients tend to grasp at the psychological perspective as if it were a bag of emergency survival tools when there is chaos, uncertainty or a morass of incomprehensible reactions they need to figure out. At such times their instinctive reaction is usually to re-impose more control. For me, this is their panic reaction to the surface phenomena. At this point it is better to explain to clients what is really happening from a psychological point of view. This is illustrated in Table 1.1.

Table 1.1   Business reality and psychological reality

Business reality	Psychological reality
Plan	Register events
Fix problems	Understanding as an action
Speed up processes	Go slower to speed up
Be proactive	Walk minefields
Legitimate	Not yet legitimate

AN INDIVIDUAL APPROACH TO OD

Having an individual approach to OD still allows me to make use of all the frameworks and ways of thought that I learned from others. In addition to the structure of 'roles played by OD people' I also describe four principles of my own which underpin everything I do in OD. For the most part they do differ slightly from the approach of those who taught me.

A Bottom-up Approach as Well as a Top-down Approach

My own approach is far more of a bottoms-up approach than other OD people. For example, Ed Schein's view is that "The setting chosen should be as near the top of the organisation or client system as possible" (Schein, 1998, p. 132). I am joined by a few others such as Shaw (1997) who argues that change agents are well advised to empower lower-levels (Gallos, 2006, p. 66). The approach I take is bottom up PLUS top down. Dick Beckhard, in his definition specifies that an OD intervention is a "top down" affair. However, in conversation with him he would refer to himself as a "trade union rep" i.e., that he was representing middle management vis-à-vis senior management. By bottom-up I mean that the troops or middle management can take action without it necessarily being sanctioned by the 'top' but it is in line with what the organisation wants. I mean by this not just business as usual activities, where the troops taking initiative is simply a question of empowerment, but I mean that are the troops creating some kind of change in the organisation or prompting something which the 'top' will eventually support (but I do not mean skunk works) because I get top-down support as well.

Simplicity

This principle is implicit in all the seven roles of OD. This emphasis is in contrast to many OD people who advocate that, since the world has become more complex, our OD tools and frameworks should also become more complex. I go the other way and believe that, because of the complexity in the world, all the more reason for providing managers with what is simple.

My first brush with the principle of simplicity came from Professor Lotte Bailyn of MIT in a course she was teaching for the PhD students on research methods. This principle she espoused by claiming that we should always choose the simplest method for analyzing data, and the simplest method for showing the results. I have followed the principle ever since.

Being is as Important as Doing

This principle is also illustrated in all the seven roles. To me this is the sine qua non of OD. I emphasise it relatively more than my teachers do, without taking away from the fact that it was also a principle for them. For me the inner psyche is key. Maybe being is even more important than doing.

Content as Well as Process is Important for OD

Here I drift away a little from Ed Schein's teachings and writing. It will be apparent through the seven roles that I am inputting more text on content than process than many OD people would be comfortable with. Ed Schein emphasises this dichotomy frequently in his work stating at one point that we should be aware of "the relative attention given to the content of the work and the structure of the organisation versus the process by which work is done and the structure of that process ... " (Schein, 1989, p. 178). His point is that managers focus too much on content than process and refers to his approach to OD as 'process consultation'.

Where I am coming from
The four principles give you an idea of 'where I am coming from', The roles, and their names, will help to guide you through the book as well. Most of the book consists in describing seven roles OD people play. These roles were derived from asking myself the question "What do I do?" until I felt complete. They were not derived from reading the literature.

THE ROLES

In total, I set out 7 roles though, of course, there may be more: The Seer, Translator, Cultivator, Catalyst, Navigator, Teacher and Guardian. I would not want the reader to interpret these as "The" seven roles set in stone. Maybe it will encourage you to work out your own.

In each role, there consists of a basic explanation, exploration of the role, the role's approach to change and then some practical tools: books to read, and OD tools. It is structured that way so that you have more of a practical focus than an academic focus. I have written down the role as it works for me, in order to help you do what OD people do.

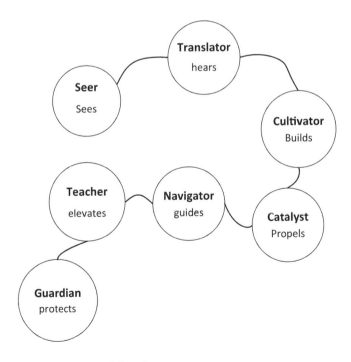

Figure 1.1   Map of the 7 OD roles

THE CHAPTERS

The Introduction and Chapter 1 describe the basic stance of the book so you can get your bearings.

Chapter 2 describes a role called the *Seer*. Rather than being magical, it describes the very ordinary skill of seeing things; of seeing through appearances and looking into the future. Some people are better able to predict things than others. This is one of the skills of the Seer. The guru I associate with this is Ed Schein.

The third chapter is about a role called the *Translater*. To some extent this is about the hearing equivalent to seeing. But the Translater has its own tack: it listens, but listens in order to translate one person to another. Also, it listens to the organisation's 'speech'. The Translator is looking for the purpose behind problems in the organisation because there are no such things as problems, only intentions and purpose. The guru I associate with this is David Cooperrider.

Chapter 4 is about the *Cultivator*. This role understands a great variety of things. Most important would be understanding rhythm and pacing in the organisation; when to go slow and being able to go slow, as well as recognizing when to operate at great speed. The Cultivator is sometimes called the Doctor and aims at healing people and the organisation. They focus on assumptions of wellness not sickness in the organisation. The guru I associate with this role is Ed Nevis.

Chapter 5 is about the *Catalyst*. This is a high energy dynamic role. It can interchange with the Cultivator role if you monitor yourself as an OD person. The Catalyst knows how to hit the bulls eye, is good at combining different things or people to create something quite new and exciting. The guru I associate with this role is Dick Beckhard.

Chapter 6 is called the *Navigator*. This is the role that charts people and the organisation through psychological space. It is an interesting role because it is often not done well in organisations. It means knowing the direction, the current space as well as propelling people to get to the direction. The guru I associate with this role is Peter Senge.

Chapter 7 is the *Teacher*. This role goes way beyond imparting knowledge or information but elevating functioning. This role does not refer to learning, being in a double-loop learning mode (Argyris and Schon, 1996). It turns this mode of thinking around to teaching well not learning well. The guru I associate with this is Otto Scharmer.

Chapter 8 describes the *Guardian*. This role concerns itself with creating an ethical not just an effective organisation. This chapter describes what an organisation would look like if it were full of faith, hope and charity. Part of this role is being aware of oneself, and having disciplines to encourage that. The guru I associate with this role is Warner Burke.

CHAPTER 2

THE SEER

THE BASICS OF THE SEER ROLE

An OD consultant I know was hired because she could always predict what was going to happen in the organisation. Likewise, in running a workshop she could predict what would happen. She was always correct.

Another OD consultant always knew when someone wanted to ask a question but not from any observable or audible signal that they wanted to ask a question. He was always correct.

Both are being Seers. When I am working as an OD consultant or adviser, everything I do involves or requires the Seer. This is, also, the role that OD people tend to play most easily and thoughtfully. It is the most recognizable of the seven roles I describe. Often, it is the most legitimate OD role. One client I worked for over five years hired me for that role of Seer. It was expressed in weekly meetings with them for example, as well as other pieces of work. During those meetings I would counsel my clients on what was 'really going on' in their organisation. They could rarely see it and often misinterpreted different events or reactions in the organisation. I was paid to 'see' or perceive beyond the surface reality to the psychological state of the company. This required that I work with content not just OD process. We were engaged with a great deal of change in the organisation and interpreting the ebbs and flows of that change was the meat of our conversations. There was no question that there was a *perceptual* difference between us. To some extent this arises not from some innate superiority but from being an 'outsider'. (Professor John Hunt of London Business School would frequently refer to us both as 'marginals' reflecting the idea of being an outsider. What John was referring to was that he was from Australia and I from NZ. However, the key point was that that was why we were both hired to do and say what we did.)

I think many OD people do the same kind of thing. All I am doing is calling it a specific role.

What do Seers do?

What do Seers do? They can see the invisible, see around corners and see through because they are perceptive, can predict. In short they see through the obvious and through appearances. It is about perception.

While it is possible to manage business opportunities with a clear purpose in mind, it is not possible to manage or plan one's way through or around a psychological concern. The skills required in dealing with psychological reality are perceptual and attentive. The role is that of Seer.

There is no question that different people perceive things differently. One of my favourite courses in my first degree was a Psychology one on Perception. We did all manner of experiments testing the perception of people in the class. The most interesting experiment involved the perception of time. In other words, figuring out how much time had elapsed while various background incidents occurred. The pinnacle of the experiment tested how long we estimated a minute had passed while various forms of music were played. The best music for most of us for predicting time was classical. When that music was being played, most of us were close to the actual minute mark when we said that a minute was up. Aside from those interesting times, it was clear that some people were good at perception and others not. I think OD people are good at it in unstructured situations. When a situation becomes very structured, OD people tend to become bored and switch off and their innate perception doesn't work in the same way. It remains the case, however, that the focus of their perception is to see beyond appearances.

Living in my own Reality

At one point in my OD career I decided to take a job i.e., become an employee instead of being my own boss. At first it was a complete disaster and I wondered what I had done. My fellow employees and I lived in two completely different psychological worlds. I couldn't see what they saw and I couldn't hear what they heard, literally. I could go through a meeting, hyper conscious that I wasn't taking anything in and, by the end, was unable to recall a word. What interested them was simply different. It proved to me forcefully, that as an OD person, there really were separate roles that you acted out. There is, in other words, a 'business reality' where most people live, and a psychological reality, where I lived. And where, I think, most OD people live.

DISSONANCE

The primary psychological skill in the Seer is seeing through: knowing that there is a dissonance between what seems to be happening and what actually is going on psychologically. Paying attention to dissonance occurs in our everyday life, especially when there is confusion, when what is said isn't what is meant, or where someone is suspected of having a hidden agenda. All these are everyday signs we use to inform ourselves that something 'else' is going on. Moreover, in these situations, we assume that what is invisible is more truthful and real than what is on the surface. Witness the labels 'real' and 'actual'. This is our psychological sense at work and it is only by stepping into this psychological reality that we can figure out what's going on. Psychological reality is intruding when problems have been around for a long time, when there is a strong feeling that we have been here before.

Schein (1988, 1999) links this with what I am calling 'psychological reality'. For example: "Many of the forces that influence the outcome of relationships are hidden and/or hard to decipher. To become a more effective helper requires not only a greater ability to see and hear what is going on, in order to detect and decipher these hidden forces, but also a greater personal flexibility in responding to them. One of the most important functions of process consultation is to make visible that which is invisible" (Schein, 1999, p. 84).

MINDFULNESS

One psychological factor that seems related to the Seer is Mindfulness and Mindlessness, as spoken and written by Ellen Langer of Harvard Ed School. I was lucky enough to take part in a seminar from Ellen Langer at MIT. She described the difference between mindfulness, which is focused on processing information by meaning, and mindlessness which processes information by its structure. She talked of one of her experiments. She had set it up so that different people would come to a photocopier, obviously to photocopy something. The experiment revolved around gaining access to use this photocopier and determining the cognitive process going on in the people being asked. The experimenters waited near one and approached people already using it and asked "whether they would let us copy something" (Langer, 1989, p. 14). However, they gave different reasons. Some were intelligent and some were not. There were three types of reasons: "Excuse me, may I use the Xerox machine?"; "Excuse me may I use the Xerox machine because I want to make copies?"; "Excuse me, may I use the Xerox machine because I'm in a rush?" (Langer, 1989, p. 14).

The first and second reasons have the same 'content'. In other words, the meaning is the same. People who are processing in terms of meaning would relate to these two requests as if they were the same. "Structurally, however, they are different". This is because the first does not have a 'reason'. However, the last two reasons are similar because the structure of the sentence is the same (they both have a reason). "If people comply with the last two requests in equal numbers this implies attention to structure rather than conscious attention to content. This, in fact, was what we found. There was more compliance when a reason was given – whether the reason sounded legitimate or silly. People responded mindlessly to the familiar framework rather than mindfully attending to the content" (Langer, 1989, p. 15).

The Seer role corresponds to the meaningful behaviour because it relates to seeing through the obvious, and relating to content or meaning not structure.

THE SEER IS THE REALIST

In psychological reality it is the Seer who is the realist and pragmatist: the business focused manager is the mystical wishful thinker. Thus the task for the OD person is describing to the line what is going on in psychological reality so that they can understand why there are impasses at the level of business reality. In short, the key contribution of the Seer is to see, recognize, know and describe psychological reality.

Being able to explain why events are occurring often requires describing one person's reality to another in order for both to feel sane, instead of seeing the other person as mad or wholly unreasonable. In the psychological realm, this type of interpretation may be a sufficient act to transform the concern enough for it to no longer create business problems. Within the rules of psychological reality simple comprehension often is an act sufficient unto itself.

THE SEER

- Sees through appearances
- Sees around corners
- Predicts the future
- Knows what is 'really going on'
- Sees the figure/ground
- Sees beyond the obvious
- Understands and processes meaning

THE DYNAMIC OF FIGURE/GROUND

Managers usually attend to many things. The Seer focuses on only those things that are a priority at the moment. You may wonder how they do this.

One way of understanding the Seer is with the Gestalt concept of figure/ground (Mann, 2010, p. 11). This refers to a perceptual phenomenon that is to do with what you pay attention to. The figure/ground tells you what you should pay attention to in order for the overall processes in the organisation to function at their best. Managers can focus and prioritise quite well yet still not be doing the right things. It is the 'figure' we should focus on or prioritise at any one moment, and the 'ground' which is context.

If you were traveling along in a car, idly looking at the landscape, your attention might, first of all, notice a bird in flight. At this point, the bird would be the 'figure' and everywhere else in that landscape is 'ground'. The perception alters after a while, however. Soon, another object in the landscape, a tree, comes to your attention. The bird is no longer 'figure'; it is now 'ground'. The tree is now the figure. Nothing has changed in the landscape except your own perception making first the bird and secondly a tree, the figure. Again, as you travel further along in the car, the sun comes to your attention. This becomes the 'figure' and the tree, along with the bird fade into the background and become 'ground'.

We should have a good reason to notice the bird. Perhaps what makes it highlighted is that it is in motion. Or, it might be its vivid colours, its goal-directed flight. The tree should surface and 'emerge' from the background by virtue of a feature such as its height, the picturesque display of its branches or the colour of its leaves.

The current or 'live' figure/ground suggests that there is an alive aspect to a person, object or event which tells you what you should be attending to. If you do not do so soon enough, you have to deal with matters on an urgent basis. If you downplay the importance of current figures then you will be attending to crises more than you should.

MACADAMIA NUTS

A colleague runs a business growing, shelling, processing and selling macadamia nuts. It has the largest processing plant in Australasia. When he first bought it, with a partner, they imagined they could get it going as a reasonably successful operation. The costs of running it proved, in the end, to be very high and they subdivided the large orchard into smaller units which were bought up by four others. The idea was to have those others pick the nuts but everybody's processing would be done by a central unit still owned by my colleague and his partner. This transaction proved to be highly lucrative and the Macadamia business still runs in this manner.

I was asked to consult for them for a fee of providing me with dinner. Neither had run a business before. The situation had involved massive risk but, by their decision, they managed to get their original capital back out of the business and sit on a lot more. The risk was then spread over a wider group of people.

What is Going on Here?

The role required was that of a Seer. The issue is perceptual. The skills required are largely those relating to managing a figure/ground relationship. (See Polster et al, 1974, who states "figure/ground reversibility is at the root of fluidity in life", p. 33). It involved a switch from 'growing then processing', to 'processing and then growing'. Unless you can follow or anticipate the switch in figure/ground you will miss the business opportunity. Initially, processing is ground but later it is figure.

Psychological Reality

When we are working in psychological reality, there often is a need to detect what should be highlighted as a psychological fact to which we need to pay attention. Metaphorically speaking, we need a system that answers the question "which psychological concern is now at the forefront, ringing alarm bells?" This is explained by the figure/ground concept.

The relationship between figure and ground is constantly changing, whether we are watching a landscape or an organisation. Our perceived environment, which determines our behaviour, is in constant motion.

ON NOT SEEING THE FIGURE FOR THE GROUND

A Sales Manager in the UK took five hours in a feedback session in a Development Centre I had created. The other Managers took anything from 2 to 4 hours. If something like this occurs there can be only one explanation, given that he was not stupid. He, or the feedback giver, must have been focused on 'ground' not 'figure'. No feedback session should last that long. It was partly because he insisted on drawing the discussion over and over again to business problems, when you should temporarily suspend them and focus on yourself and your behaviour. Business problems are there as the context for the issues being talked about, but are not the figure.

An example of focusing on figure not ground was the feedback session that lasted 2 hours, within the same set of managers. This was a Sales manager whose sales unit often performed the best. His level of education was one of the lowest in this particular set of managers. Nevertheless he was in many ways the smartest. He had chosen, deliberately, the best salesmen and knew how to motivate them. He focused on the few key right things. He knew which clients to visit with his salesmen and which to leave alone. As I left that office, I was aware of the leadership effect. I felt, as presumably did his team, lifted up and filled with energy, as if I could do anything. These are signs that he was able to focus on figure not ground, or none of these events would occur.

Recognition and Pattern Awareness

Thus the Seer role. Within this frame, we need to be able to pay attention to psychological forces in a way that maps trends and movement, prevents overload and calls attention to places where there is a problem. This will occur when the figure and ground relationship shifts and one psychological aspect recedes while another moves to the foreground. While this process is no different than the one which brings a particular business issue to the foreground, what is different are the skills including recognition and pattern awareness.

RESOLVING THE FIGURE

The first thing a Seer knows is that the particular psychological concern which is foreground at the moment must be resolved before it will fade back and become background. Before one can productively move onwards, a good Seer knows that a figure must be attended to. Otherwise we will be tripped up by the fact that these psychological priorities have a mind of their own. If our attention skips a concern or avoids one, it nevertheless will, in psychic space, remain figure. To move through psychological reality too fast because one 'doesn't have time' simply means that one has wasted time. Even though one may be working frantically hard within business reality one will not move at all if a preeminent psychological reality is put off. Eventually the anchor that is the psychological realm will become a frustrating millstone weighing down progress. Unseen but definitely felt.

A Seer will know what to begin to prioritise or pay attention to. They may know before others do, what needs to be focused on.

RUNNING AN EMPOWERMENT WORKSHOP

I once ran a series of Empowerment workshops for a large manufacturing company in the UK. In an earlier contract I had with this same company, I had been rehired for work on the business/ cultural plans of the businesses for no other reason than my Seer role. This was explicit from my client. Some of this role related simply to deciphering the group dynamic in the various groups we worked with.

One of the empowerment two- day events was with the HR Division. This group were seen by the rest of the organisation as the main obstacle to change in the organisation and the business managers in the business units that I had been working with had impressed upon me the urgency and importance of reading the riot act to them and stopping their bureaucratic behaviours and rules. The group was a bit tricky but basically it was going the way I wanted it, trusting to psychological reality and, in particular the Seer. Nevertheless, they had descended to arguments and chaos by the end of the first day. This didn't bother me as I knew we would be OK on the second day. This required the Seer to see through appearances and 'see through the obvious'. I did, however, get a tongue lashing from the boss of the HR group who told me that everything was a mess and I didn't know what I was doing. On the contrary, I knew exactly what I was doing. On the second day everything came right as any Seer would have known. I was flabbergasted that a boss of an HR division couldn't suss out the dynamic of the group better. If you are an OD person, I am sure you would already have known too; that is why I have included the Seer as an OD role.

MODEL OF CHANGE FOR THE SEER

The model of *change* I use for the Seer is based on Will Schutz's three-dimensional theory of interpersonal behaviour (Schutz, 1966, 1984). I use this model to give me content not just process. It is one that can be used in depth as well as superficially. It helps the Seer put names to processes that are fluid and intangible and helps you be precise and well-aimed. It explains how to interpret what you SEE or are aware of.

His theory can be used in many levels. His theory states that three core areas of experience exist in any interaction between individuals: namely inclusion, control and openness (formerly affection). In relation to individuals, the inclusion area of experience describes the frequency and style of one's interaction with others, as well as how one establishes an identity alongside others. The control area describes that area of experience related to exerting influence and establishing effectiveness. Openness describes the manner of direct engagement with others, and with the way in which relationships are sustained.

Using Will's psychological theory, you can label what you see and interpret it in a way that is helpful (Schein, 2012). The Seer is engaged because, to use the model, you have to notice things in the first place (that 'people pay attention to others', for example). However, instead of noticing only that 'people pay attention to others' the Seer knows that this is relevant in terms of 'inclusion'. We know that this 'means something': that the individual has a sense of their own significance, that he/she is likely to be good at claiming space, and so on.

The change model of the Seer goes further. This is because you can predict what will happen (the Seer) by the phases of the model. You can predict the next psychological phase. For example, when a group forms, everyone is concerned with establishing an identity for themselves vis-à-vis others. They are focused on interacting with each other in a general manner and they establish norms for interaction. Once they have resolved these inclusion issues to some extent they move onto the second phase, which is focused on resolving the control issues. Here the group determines a pattern of authority they are comfortable with, who is in or out of control, how to set tasks so that people feel efficacious (able to achieve goals). Again, when and until the group is satisfied that these control issues are resolve to a reasonable degree, they move to the third phase where they focus on openness issues. This means they pay attention to issues like how close and personal they will be with one another, what the nature of relationships will be and so on. This model is a little like the Forming, Storming, Norming, Performing model. A group cannot start at the openness phase, for example. Nor can it jump straight from the inclusion phase to the openness phase.

These phases enable you to predict (Seer) what any group will be focused on ahead of time.

You can use this model for almost anything. In what follows I have laid it out so it guides you during change. In this context, it is critical for the Seer to be able to discriminate what psychological reality is, not just to know that 'something' is happening. In other words they need to label it. This makes the Seer an 'expert' as well as a 'process' consultant.

GETTING ANOTHER PERSPECTIVE; SIGNS TO SEE

Will Schutz' model I use as a Seer, to decipher what is really going on in a group of people or an organisation as a whole. Table 2.1 sets out one way to use the model.

The difference between this and other OD models is the knowledge comes as much from the observer as the actor. In other words, the expertise is as much in the Seer as the manager. Seers need this extra knowledge. You can use this model easily.

Table 2.1   Signs Seers can use to monitor change

	Signs that all is well	Signs that all is not well
inclusion	People pay attention to others, are interested in what they say; people are up, alert; alive; people walk with a spring in their step; you feel energized; atmosphere is positive; people are very aware of possibilities; what to hope for	People are oblivious to others and miss what they say; people cannot understand the meaning of what was said; people are bored and boring; energy; tired or lackluster; negative view of future; people interrupt each other
control	General atmosphere of everything working smoothly; atmosphere is of confidence; people are embarking on tests they look forward to rather than hard work; feel as if you can do anything you put your mind to; feel as if everything will 'work'; can-do	General atmosphere of things being impossible; boasting macho behaviour; everything is difficult; nothing runs smoothly; people drop things; feel as if you will be stopped once you have embarked in things; hampered by past failure; full of themselves or timid
openness	General atmosphere of being fulfilled, purposeful because people feel that what they are doing matters; and that it is all right to be yourself; there may be times of stillness within even if busy; relationships are sustained; fun	General atmosphere of emptiness or overwhelmed with a business agenda that allows for nothing else; games played; political; cruel and brutal; people avoid dealing with things in depth; avoidance generally; frantic activity at times; no sense of purpose

Source: Adapted from FIRO theory by Dr. Will Schutz. Used with permission of Business Consultants, Inc.

OD TOOLS TO LEAVE WITH SEERS

Books to help the Seer: Schutz. W. *The Interpersonal Underworld*; Schutz, W. *The Truth Option*; Schutz, W. *The Human Element*; Schein, E.H. *Process Consultation*, (1988); Schein, E.H., *Process Consultation Revisited* (1999).

Ed Schein and the ORJI tool

Clients/managers need to be helped to see or perceive as a Seer. One tool to help people do this is Ed Schein's ORJI tool (described in Schein 1999 p. 86). This is designed to help two people in a relationship, understand what is going on in that relationship. "The most important thing to understand in any relationship is what goes on *inside the head, especially one's own head"* (Schein, 1999 p. 86 italics the author's).

There are four steps in the ORJI tool. That is, "we observe (O), we react emotionally to what we have observed (R), we analyze, process and make judgments based on observations and feelings (J), and we behave overtly in order to make something happen – we intervene (I)" (Schein, 1999, p. 86). If you follow this sequence you will be managing yourself in a more perceptive manner. You will become more aware of what you are noticing and more accurate in your perceptions. For Reactions: "In our culture we … learn that feelings should not influence judgements; that feelings are a source of distortion, and we are told not to act impulsively on our feelings. But, paradoxically, we often end up acting *most* on our feeling" (Schein, 1999, p. 88). Schein's argument is that we are better off being aware of our feelings rather than unaware of them (cf. the Seer), because then we have a choice whether to act on those feelings. Judgment is about deciding on some course of action. "This ability to analyse prior to action is what makes humans capable of planning sophisticated behavior to achieve complex goals and sustain action chains that take us years into the future". (Schein, 1999, p. 89). Intervention occurs after we have decided on some course of action, i.e. come to some sort of judgement. Schein considers the most important steps in this process are the first ones, the ones closest to the Seer behaviour.

Ellen Langer's Mindfulness

Another tool that can be used for OD is Ellen Langer's work, especially her book on Mindfulness. Her book is designed to keep you open to possibility. Much of the time our behaviour is mindless. Mindfulness is not the sort framed as Buddhist meditation but something different. She argues for us to be open to actively noticing things (the Seer). She argues that just "as mindlessness is the rigid reliance of old categories, mindfulness means the continual creation of new ones … A mindful state also implies openness to new information. Like category making, the receiving of new information is a basic function of living creatures" (Langer, 1989, p. 63 and 66).

Gary Hamel: The Future of Management

I have classified Gary as a Seer because anyone who has seen him teach or consult will know he is born to teach you to see through the obvious. One of his roles is the Seer. He also challenges organisations and senior managers to be Seers.

These are almost the first words of his *Future of Management* book. " … I'd like to pose a question: Who's managing your company? You might be tempted to answer, 'the CEO', or 'the executive team', or 'all of us in middle management'. And you'd be right, but that wouldn't be the whole truth. To a large extent, your company is being managed right now by a small coterie of long-departed theorists and practitioners who invented the rules and conventions of 'modern' management back in the early years of the 20ᵗʰ century. They are the poltergeists who inhabit the musty machinery of management. It is their edicts, echoing across the decades, that invisibly shape the way your company allocates resources … and makes decisions" (Hamel, 2007, p. ix).

20 QUESTIONS

Who are the Seers in your organisation? ....

....

When are you most a Seer? ....

....

Are you in your own perceptual world? ....

....

What skills do you have most as a Seer? ....

....

How do others behave when you are a Seer? ....

....

Do you like what you see as a Seer? ....

....

How did you come to be a Seer? ....

....

Do you like being a Seer? ....

....

Do you have Seers around you? ....

....

What is it like when you are with other Seers? ….................…………………………

....

Do you regard the Seer as the classic OD role? ....

....

Do you consciously use the figure/ground dynamic? ....

....

Can you predict the future? ....

....

Are you known for being perceptive? ....

....

Is your organisation well, in terms of the Schutz model ....

....

Is your organisation stuck in any of the Schutz phases? ....

....

In terms of change, where does the organisation most need to focus? ....

....

Where does the organisation most need to direct its energies? ....

....

Where do you feel most exuberant as a Seer? ....

....

How can you develop yourself best as a Seer? ....

....

EXERCISES

The following section gives you some exercises to practice to be a Seer. You can do them as an employee or manager, student or as an OD consultant.

- **Exercise One**: Write a case study using your own organisation as an example. Write a descriptive view of it not a prescriptive view, as if to give to an outsider. Write it, that is, in neutral. Leave it alone without looking at it for a few days and then go back to study it. What is the figure(s) you are paying attention to? What is the ground you are not paying attention to. What figure and ground should you be paying less attention to/ more attention to?
- **Exercise Two**: Practice at the next meeting to watch for facial expressions, where people sit, who interrupted others, what the body gestures are, and so on. After you have emerged from the meeting, figure out what was 'really going on' at the meeting.
- **Exercise Three**: Use a figure/ ground visual to predict what will happen in the near future. Start by simply comparing the objects which are 'figures' with daily reality. Remember there is a business reality and a psychological reality. You can have both but greater knowledge of the latter means you understand the psychic underworld of the organisation better.
- **Exercise Four**: Using the Schutz model, work out what phase your organisation is in, and what phase your immediate team is in. If you are a consultant, think of your partners and network. What are the key issues to enhance (strengths) and work on (challenges).
- **Exercise Five**: Work out a practice exercise for 'seeing'. The objective here is to see if people really do see. Have a volunteer in your group go out the door, come back in knocking on the door. He/she walks to a predetermined place. He comes up to one person in the left-behind group and shakes hands. That's the exercise. You need to be the facilitator. Ask the rest of the group: "what they saw" and write down everything they say on a white board. You will struggle to hear anything said that was like a Seer. You will hear interpretations like "she was unhappy", "she went too fast", "she was too hesitant knocking on the door". All of these are interpretations and evaluations not pure observation. Discussion point at the end: how are performance appraisals done? Like this? what does that mean?

Table 2.2   Rate your own skill as a Seer

	1 Awful	2 Poor	3 Adequate	4 Good	5 Superb
See into the future					
See through things/people					
Perceptive					
See the figure/ ground					
Can adjust the figure/ ground					

Total out of 25=

Table 2.3   Rate your colleagues or team as Seers

	1 Awful	2 Poor	3 Adequate	4 Good	5 Superb
See into the future					
See through things/people					
Perceptive					
See the figure/ground					
Can adjust the figure ground					

Total out of 25=

Table 2.4   Get someone else to rate your skills as a Seer

	1 Awful	2 Poor	3 Adequate	4 Good	5 Superb
See into the future					
See through things/people					
Perceptive					
See the figure/ground					
Can adjust the figure/ground					

Total out of 25=

CHAPTER 3

THE TRANSLATOR

HEARING WHAT IS REALLY BEING SAID

Another classic role of OD is to hear what is *really* being said. This includes hearing what is not being said. However, it is also to translate what has been said or not said to other people. Hence the name Translator not Hearer to refer to this chapter. Even further, from my perspective the role includes the art of hearing what the organisation is 'saying' not just what an individual is saying. This is a tool for a systems perspective. Notice that I am not referring to literally 'hearing better'. You could be half-deaf and still be a Translator.

TELLING THE TRUTH

One of my mentors was Will Schutz, one of the gurus in the Human Potential movement. I remember one workshop I was on with Will leading. All 30 of us were seated in an enormous circle. He asked us all a question related to what we wanted to do in a session of the workshop, and then he went around and asked each of us individually whether we wanted to do what he said. We were allowed to say 'Yes' or 'No' and nothing else. Slowly the process continued with each person saying yes or no. Everyone said 'yes'. Or had they? Will proceeded to point out three people who had not really said 'yes' even though they had mouthed the word 'yes'. One way or another they had indicated by body movement or voice tone that they didn't really agree with his proposal at all. All three admitted, when asked, that they did not, in fact, agree with Will's original proposal. The Translator hears these subtle aspects of the OD role. Basically, it means that people do not always tell the truth. However, some people, the Translators, hear this. In the example with Will, there were a couple of others who also heard, like Will, that not everybody had told the truth when they answered the original question Will posed.

HEARING WHAT HAS NOT BEEN SAID

Hearing what has not been said is harder than monitoring voice tone. A consultant and I had the honour of being the first consultants to be hired for an away-day workshop with the Manexec team at a UK company (the senior exec committee). We even had some of the Board's Japanese managers accompanying us as well as the company's guardian of compliance issues.

One of the sub-agendas we, the consultants, wanted to know about was the true legal status of the company and the relationship between the company hiring us (A) and their 'strategic partner' (B), which had Japanese managers on the Board. We needed to know because it had never been presented or explained clearly, so we were intent on asking about it.

It had been explained to us as a joint venture (between the two companies). Imagine our surprise when we finally cornered one of the legal experts in one of our pre-workshop interviews. He told us that B fully owned A. We sat there, unable to speak for several seconds. "So A is fully owned, bought outright". "Yes, that's right" and along the table he pushed the appropriate legal documentation towards us, to prove it.

What is going on here? What was the OD role which meant that both a marketing/ strategy specialist (my colleague) and an OD/ psychology specialist (me) had exactly the same need to find out a piece of information. It was the lack of clarity that pushed us both to the Translator role. Something had not been said. What we could decipher simply propelled us to make sure we heard.

What did we find out that hardly anyone else knew? That organisation A does not legally exist. No one else knows this but the CE and the legal and compliance experts. None of the other managers, who we interacted with regularly, had been told.

TRANSLATING EACH OTHER TO EACH OTHER

The skill of the Translator is also to explain people to other people, to translate their actions as well as words; a major component of my work as an OD consultant.

I once 'translated' two managers in a client of mine who experienced a great deal of mutual conflict. One man was an ex-SAS officer and he was in charge of systems and IT. The other man was the Finance Director and the effective MD in the organisation. Their conflict had got to such a pitch that the Finance Director asked me to sit in the middle of them and try and resolve some of it. They started off reasonably amicably but then descended into their normal disputatious style.

At one stage the ex-SAS man visibly crumpled and 'shrank' into his body. The Finance Director was known to be a bully and even though his colleague had 'crumpled', he carried on blitzing him. My role was to intervene and translate one to another to try to bring some rationality into the discussion. The task was always to find the MEANING of what each person had said rather than the structure of what had been said. Another key task was to get yourself out of the way and, critically, to distance yourself from your likes and dislikes of the people concerned. In the above example, I actually liked the Finance Director even though he was a bully and didn't particularly like the ex-SAS man who I regarded as boring. But my interventions were more to shore up the latter and stall the former.

Every Translator will have been in the situation of saying to one person "What he/she means is this … " and then interpreting after that to the other person: "what she/he means is this … ". It helps to be the kind of person to process information by meaning or content and not by structure, as we saw in Chapter 1 (in relation to Ellen Langer 1989).

People decide things for their own reasons. The translator hears what this is about. They hear the original intention or need being expressed by the individual. This provides a way out of log jams, by hearing meaning. When someone is heard, animosity or friction often disappears.

HEARING VOICES: RESISTANCE TO CHANGE

In the psychological mind set, resistance to change, for example, is interpreted, as a working assumption, as an intelligent response. The stance of a good Translator is this: If we assume that the behaviour we're witnessing is positively intentioned, we should look for the intelligence within the message that is sent.

Understanding resistance requires you to 'hear voices' or, in other words, hear what is REALLY being said. The latter is hearing the meaning of information rather than the structure of information. Figure 3.1 demonstrates some examples of resistant voices that you can translate. The bracketed voice is what is really being said. All of them are positively intentioned towards the organisation in spite of the fact that there is 'resistance'.

LETTING PEOPLE SPEAK

One key aspect of the Translator is to *allow* people to speak; an age-old dimension of the OD role. One of my favourite clients was a rather poor ramshackle company in the retail industry in the UK. They had just been bought out by a consortium

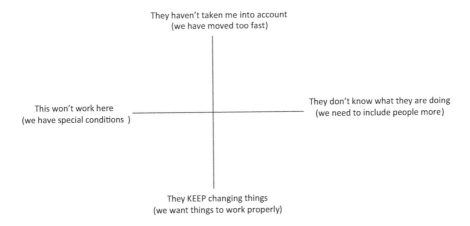

Figure 3.1   Hearing voices; interpreting resistance to change

and had as their context a financially precarious situation. The managers were up against it. They had to change, improve their performance or they could be fired, or the organisation could go under. The managers pretty much knew this was the state of play. Yet, in spite of this, on the workshops that I ran for them with a colleague, they moaned and moaned about their situation instead of buckling under and 'getting it'. We decided to allow the moaning to occur from Monday am to Tuesday lunch time and then we would stop it and get on with it. We judged it as essential to let some of this whingeing occur. Their agendas were each individually different. Sometimes, I would let them moan until they were themselves sick of it. The end result of all these workshops was an engaged set of managers, willing to cooperate with the change process and stepping up to the new set of behaviours expected of them in the new world. Never would this depth in engagement have been possible without letting the moaning have free rein for a while.

THE TRANSLATOR

- Hears what is really being said
- Hears what is not said
- Translates one person to another
- Lets people speak
- Understands the purpose of problems
- Processes meaning not structure
- Hears the organisation 'speaking'

THE ORGANISATION'S SPEECH

You can usually hear an individual's agenda relatively easily. You simply listen to them speaking and how they are speaking and what is not said. But how do you hear an organisation speaking?

Is it valid to do so? Yes. By virtue of events not working well. By the change process stalling and so forth. These are examples of the organisation's speech rather than individual's speech. Someone who is skilled at this kind of translation will be aware of needs, states, wishes within the organisation-as-a-whole, and be able to hear these as messages. In other words, they act as if the organisation were speaking.

We can apply this same skill to the organisation and try to interpret what it needs to do 'to get its voice heard', to 'get its message across'. Here the purpose of the Translator is to hear, understand, and interpret the organisation's speech.

The Meaning of Getting Ill/Problems

When we get ill, we often sit back and attempt to understand what the reaction means, what the symptom is saying in a larger context. It is common to understand physical illness as representing a message of the body. It is saying something more than 'I've got a headache". In addition, it is saying "I'm working too hard" Or, "I need to slow down". We tend to automatically think this way in interpreting the malfunctioning of our bodies. We think of ourselves as a whole, so the body's reactions are interpreted in an overarching context and meaning is attributed to an otherwise counterproductive occurrence. Pain is assumed to have a positive, not a negative, intent. Thus, resistance to change is a vital interpretive sign that is being spoken by our body to help us assist it in changing.

Pain Messages from the Organisation

The same is true in organisations. Pain messages need to be translated as if they were one of the main languages which the organisation speaks. Instead of getting frustrated with this foreign language, it is necessary to acknowledge that the pain is (or can be heard of as) a language which can be understood. Of course, you can never understand this language directly. It must be translated. Understanding will not be helped by yelling back, or by speaking louder, much as we do to foreigners who do not speak our language. We may not bother talking to a foreigner who sounds like they are speaking gibberish, but we do not thereby automatically assume that such a person is irrational or unintelligent.

This is not to say that listening to an organisation speak in such a manner is easy. Our normal human reactions interfere, both with our hearing and with our interpretation of this speech. But this is no different than one's frustration with one's own body when it resists with its headache, forcing one to stop doing what you were intently set on doing.

Thus the key contribution of the Translator is to *hear within psychological reality*.

THE PURPOSE OF PROBLEMS

Within psychological reality, anything that, from the business perspective, might be considered a hindrance is treated by a Translator instead as constructive and purposive. For example, problems are not examined in order to find their cause; they are examined to find their intent. In psychological/ OD space, problems aren't problems. Rather, they are messages to be attended to, indicators pointing the way forward. To perform this valuable function, problems need not only to be seen but listened to and understood. As indicated, problems are not things that illustrate what is wrong, they are signs to what is right. They are interpretive signals and to miss them is to miss the most valuable information that can be attained in OD. When things go wrong from a business perspective, they, in psychic reality, must be approached as underlying indicators, as constructive messages signalling something about the current state of the organisation. They are signals from the organisation about where it is trying to get to.

MODEL OF CHANGE FOR THE TRANSLATOR

Translators are particularly attuned to hearing different agendas which may coincide or compete. One is the individual's, another is the organisation's and the third is the change agenda.

You can have the organisation-as-a-whole for or against change, for example. The organisation's agenda is not necessarily the same as the change agenda. All of these things you must be aware of as a Translator. One of Dick Beckhard's main teaching points to me was that, as an OD consultant, the agenda you are responsive to is the organisation's agenda first, not the individual's (including your paymaster). It is by doing this that you have a systems perspective.

Scuppering the Change Agents

I once worked for a company in the UK as an OD consultant alongside a team of process reengineering consultants from a very large company. The client was very successful but faced increasing competition from US companies in its market (fund management). There were quite a few resistors around the company. I used to counsel a lot of them and virtually all were against what the process

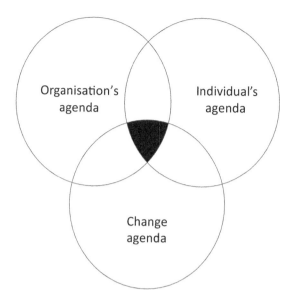

Figure 3.2   Three agendas for change

engineering company was doing. What the latter was doing was highly suspicious largely because they were so incompetent. In the model above, they carried the 'change agenda'. They intended to remove 40 per cent of the people from the small company, a figure which had not been agreed by the Board or, perhaps, anyone in management. Their overall approach was in sync with that objective. People were, however, too scared to speak openly, even to each other. They rang me to speak constantly. In this example, the resistors were the ones with the organisation's agenda in mind not the change agents. The change agents were speaking from their own agenda of ambition and securing themselves an ongoing contract. In the end, the whole exercise was scuppered because of the ludicrous nature of the consultants who misread the whole situation. The change agents were fired and the rest carried on. This outcome is not always the case. There are numerous other examples where the change is in the interest of the organisation rather than against it.

RESISTANCE PAINS AND GROWING PAINS

It helps to translate resistance pains and growing pains in terms of underlying 'problems' and their purpose and intent. Organisational pains do not sound the same depending on whether they are resistance or growing pains.

I once worked for a client in the pharmaceutical industry involved in dragging the company from the dark ages into the twentieth century. The platform I used was a series of OD workshops for the top layers of management. The managers were pretty resistant at the beginning, or cynical, but by the end were pretty enthusiastic. However, I waited, after the workshop, for their next step reaction. The managers reacted with quite a bit of dependency and blaming everyone including me. This was fine. But my clients were upset by this reaction in the managers but it was, in reality, because these managers had been treated like children and so at various times during the change process showed growing pains that manifested as resistance pains. But they are not the same thing and your OD interventions for each are quite different. Table 3.1 sets out some differences between the two.

Table 3.1   Resistance pains and growing pains

Resistance	Growing
It hurts	It hurts
No clear end goal	Can see an end goal
Trying to stop change permanently	Trying to stop change temporarily
Relates to the three agendas	Relates to the three agendas
Process is negative even if necessary	Process is positive even if necessary
Stop it	Go slower for a while

GETTING ANOTHER PERSPECTIVE: BURNOUT AS A PROBLEM AND PURPOSE

The translation of 'problem' into 'purpose' can occur in any sphere of life. Let me illustrate it in an unlikely way. I did my dissertation at MIT on the 'Effect of Personality on Burnout'. Burnout changed from being a 'problem' to being a massive 'purpose' to my life. This was so because of the results of my data collection which could only really be interpreted as 'from problem to purpose'.

I started reading about burnout to get myself out of it. It was a massive 'problem'. Nothing I read really helped, especially the research and writing that had been done in the human services. Grand claims were being made in that writing about the proneness to burnout of human service workers. Christina Maslach (1982) had published her measure of burnout, which talked of depersonalisation, emotional exhaustion and decreased personal accomplishment. None of what she wrote had any resonance with me and my exhaustion. (Years later, I spoke to her in Jerusalem at a conference symposium in Jerusalem of the International Association of Applied Psychology (IAAP) on burnout where we were both speaking. In her view, her measure of burnout should not have been published when it had been as it had been too early. However, that symposium was four years later than my time with burnout at MIT).

I started to read the few books that came from psychoanalysts or psychologists. Their clients were mostly executives and they described a very different view of burnout than the human-service oriented writers. This suggested a confounding of occupation with resulting consequences for the different 'findings' of burnout. At the time I was knee-deep in the Myers Briggs Type Indicator™ (MBTI™) (Myers et al. 2003) and used that to explain the puzzle of the burnout writing that I had encountered. There was known to be an occupational difference in MBTI™ populations. That is, human service professions were more feeling than thinking. Executives more thinking than feeling. That was as far as I got initially, but I started with that.

COMING TO THE PURPOSE

Many years later, after quite a few academic articles, I wrote one that finally got it: I called the article 'The purpose of burnout' (Garden, 1991). What this meant was that, while the experience of burnout is negative, the intent of this 'problem' is positive. This reframe in my mind was part of the Translator role. You notice the evident symptoms or 'problems' and reframe them AS IF they have positive intent. However, I didn't just have a reframe. I had my research telling me that it was very likely to be something exactly like that.

Based on my research findings, I concluded that the symptoms of burnout, which include extreme exhaustion which you cannot easily get out of and so on, were the wrong thing to concentrate on. So, what is the purpose of burnout? Greater balance in the psyche of the person. During burnout, the person's normal means of survival were clumsy and distressed. But the only way out of it was to focus on facets of the person's personality which were opposite to those facets that the person had normally identified him/herself with. The findings can summarized as follows:

1. Hostility and a lack of concern for others was associated with higher levels of burnout only for feeling types who, by definition, are supposed to have a higher concern for others. Similarly, for thinking types only, higher levels of burnout were consistently and significantly associated with lower levels of ambition or will to achieve. Theoretically, thinking types are supposed to show a higher affinity with achievement.
2. Theoretically, emotional demands should be easier for feeling types to deal with and mental demands should be easier for thinking types to deal with. Yet emotional demands predicted energy depletion for feeling types but not for thinking types. Similarly, mental demands predicted energy depletion

for thinking types but not for feeling types. In other words, burnout was most strongly associated with the kind of demand each type is *naturally adapted to deal with*.

What is Going on?

The superficial findings, that you would conclude with a 'problem-focus', were that burnout would be accompanied by the lack of use, or inability to use, the conscious function(s) which one has come to rely on as a primary tool to deal with one's world. These functions may no longer be available for use purely as a consequence of the energy depletion that marks burnout. In Jungian terms, if the psyche is deprived of energy, such as from being run down or fatigued, the conscious functions are more likely to drop in to the unconscious.

Inability to rely on the function which one has been accustomed to use for survival, for adaptation to the environment and for self-identification, would in itself be a distressing experience evoking feelings of helplessness. Getting through each day would be a struggle, one would lose one's sense of priorities. All these feelings are frequently described as intrinsic to the burnout experience. They constitute the 'problem' that is burnout. However, what is the reason/purpose/intent behind the burnout dynamic?

THE PURPOSE OF IT ALL

To explain these findings I drew upon a Jungian concept, 'enantiadromia'. "This is the emergence of the unconscious opposite in the course of time. This characteristic phenomenon practically always occurs when *an extreme one-sided tendency dominates conscious life*" (Jung, 1960, p. 262, my italics).

Psychic health is maintained by not living only out of one's conscious functions such as feeling or thinking. The psychic process called in Jungian theory, individuation, requires as an *internal demand* for adaptation and growth, that balance and wholeness are developed. If the ego thwarts this psychic demand, the unconscious may retaliate. As Jacobi (1962, p. 31) explains, "when the conscious portion of the psyche develops too one-sidedly ... it may easily land itself in a kind of hypertrophy". When this occurs for too long, it will call into action the "self-regulating mechanism of the psyche" (Jacobi, 1962, p. 38). If one has been relying too much on, or been identifying too much with, one psychic function and created an imbalance in the psyche, the unconscious may purposively pull the conscious functions down.

This theory 'explains' the findings. Too much use of the thinking function would cause, over time, the enantiadromia process. This over-use would only be possible with too many mental demands. Similarly, with a feeling type over-use of the conscious feeling function would be most likely to occur with too many emotional demands, In other words, enantiadromia seems to be a part of the burnout process.

This would imply that burnout has a positive purpose, i.e., psychic balance, and that this may be the very reason it occurs. What is the role of the Translator in this? To bring in a perspective that looks for the purpose in problems; not causes but the intent.

OD TOOLS TO LEAVE WITH TRANSLATORS

Books: Schein, E.H. 1988; Schein, E.H. 1999; Schein, E.H. 2013; Schein, E.H. 2011; Cooperrider, D. 2005; Cooperrider, D. 2006; Garden, A. 1991; Jung, C.G. 1929.

Coopenrider et al: Appreciative Inquiry

Cooperrider and colleagues have developed an approach to organisational change called Appreciative Inquiry (AI). This is a tool for Translators. It emphasizes a shift from 'problems' in organisations to their positive outcomes. Their focus is on organisational development and change. They criticize the field for problem-focused interventions. "For the most part, the interventions in OD are problem-focused or deficit-based. They start with the question "What is wrong?" It is assumed that a problem must be identified and then the appropriate intervention can be applied to 'fix' the issue" (Cooperrider et al, 2006, p. 224).

They describe another way to do OD. This way is to ask positive questions and thereby touch and create the 'positive core' of organisational life. Appreciative Inquiry operates from the premise that asking positive questions "draws out the human spirit in organizations. In a self-organizing way, the organization begins to construct a more constructive future. This is a key objective of the technique. It is accomplished by bringing forth the positive change core of the organization, making it explicit and allowing it to be owned by all" (Cooperrider et al, 2006, p. 225).

The technique follows four key phases.

- Discovery – discovering strengths and best practices
- Dream – dreaming what the organisation could be
- Design – designing the possible new organisation
- Destiny – building on the idea of the positive core to sustain itself

The AI approach is also relevant to the next chapter's role: The Cultivator.

Ed Schein's Dialogue and discussion

Another tool that is useful for Translators is Ed Schein's contrast between dialogue and discussion. He emphasizes that we are too used to discussion rather than a dialogue. To him, dialogue is a form of conversation that "starts with the assumptions that every person comes with different assumptions and that mutual understanding is in most cases an illusion. So ... we need to become more conscious of our own tacit assumptions – to recognize that others in the conversation may be operating from different assumptions" (Schein, 1999, p. 202). Discussion, on the other hand, focuses more on debate and naturally tends to not listening more than listening. In a discussion you tend to an adversarial stance. The Translator role requires an approach that is more that of dialogue than discussion.

Assagioli's Psychosynthesis

I know Assagioli for his approach to psychosynthesis and subpersonalities as well as the Inner Child and the Will. (Assagioli, 1974; Assagioli 2007; Assagioli 2012). Subpersonalities exist inside our overall personality. They react differently to different things. What we hope is that they are largely aligned but sometimes they are not and are the source of inner conflict. Working with sub-personalities is exactly the same as translating voices or hearing voices.

Assagioli is known for his approach to psychology called psychosynthesis. His aim was to create a system that 'synthesised', i.e., brought into a whole rather than simply 'analyse' as in 'psychoanalysis which breaks the personality down. Psychosynthesis builds it up. His 'egg' depicts his overall approach.

To Assagioli, the focus of our lives included the spiritual urges of people. This is expressed in the cosmic egg as a higher self or transpersonal consciousness in addition to a lower unconscious as per Freud, S. (Note that Jung had the Self). "Psychology is a psychology of the spiritual ... It denotes our highest potential" (Firman and Gila, 2002, p. 177). The higher self includes aesthetic experiences as well as spiritual. This positivity is what makes Assagioli a tool for Translators.

1) The lower unconscious

2) The middle conscious

3) The higher unconscious or superconscious

4) The field of consciousness

5) The conscious self or "I"

6) The higher self

7) The collective unconscious

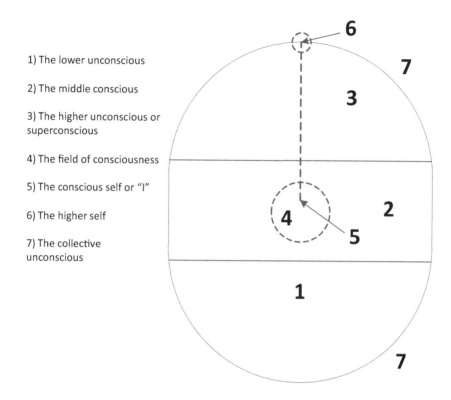

Figure 3.3   Assagioli's egg
Source: Reprinted from Psychosynthesis: A Collection of Basic Writings with permission from the Synthesis Center, Amherst, MA.

20 QUESTIONS

What are most people in your organisation not really hearing?.............................

....

Can you really hear what is being said?..

....

How do you feel when you truly hear?...

....

Do you hear the meaning of what is said, generally?..

....

Do you often disagree with what others are saying and meaning?.........................

....

Are you good at persuading others to your point of view?.....................................

....

Are you good at getting others to agree with each other?......................................

....

Do you know when something is not said?...

....

What would be better in your organisation if everyone heard what was really being said?...

....

Are people able to speak in your organisation?..

....

Are people able to hear the organisation 'speaking'?...

....

Are you able to hear the purpose behind 'problems'?...

....

Do people get impatient at the idea of hearing the organisation 'speak'?..................

....

Do people get impatient at 'problems'?..

....

Can you identify who in the organisation is good at hearing the purpose
to problems?..

....

Can you translate the voices of resistance?...

....

Can you translate the agenda of the organisation, the change and the individual?..

....

What would you most want to do to improve you as a Translator?.......................

....

Can you distinguish between growing pains and resistance pains?.......................

....

Where in the organisation can you hear that they need greater balance?...............

....

EXERCISES

The following section gives you some exercises to practice to be a Translator. You can do them as an employee, manager, student or OD consultant.

- **Exercise One**: The next time you are at a meeting, focus only on what is not being said but which should be. Remember the exercises of Will Schutz and focus on who is saying what they mean (the truth) and those who are not telling the truth. You don't need to tell anyone what you discover; it is simply learning practice and will strengthen you as a Translator
- **Exercise Two**: If you are involved with a change process and there is some discomfort (anywhere) determine first whether you are hearing resistance pains or growing pains. If it is the former, work out what they are really saying using the model in Figure 3.1. Translate their words as if they were positively intentioned to the organisation. This is what those people are REALLY saying.
- **Exercise Three**: Do you know of any group(s) of people who moan a lot? They haven't been heard. Go and listen to them and try to figure out what they are REALLY saying.
- **Exercise Four**: It is possible to hear nothing but the organisation's speech in order to effect change i.e., create the change. This is the fastest way to get change in the organisation. You need to mobilize all your strength to listen to the organisation tell you what needs to be done to create change well. What are the main messages the organisation is speaking? (write them out, as if the organisation was speaking to everyone) How would you translate these to other people who might need to hear the message? Are there different messages? If the organisation were speaking, what would it be saying at the moment? Is it speaking through an individual at a particular time, through events, through group decision? Can you interpret the messages more clearly?
- **Exercise Five**: Determine where you (or others) are on a scale of 1–10; 10 being tired and burnt out. Work out the purpose of this tiredness.

Table 3.2   Rate your own skill as a Translator

	1 Awful	2 Poor	3 Adequate	4 Good	5 Superb
Hear what is really being said					
Can translate one person's speech to another					
Hears what is not said					
Interprets the resistance speech					
Can translate the organisation's speech					

Total score out of 25=

Table 3.3   **Rate your colleagues or team as Translators**

	1 Awful	2 Poor	3 Adequate	4 Good	5 Superb
Hear what is really being said					
Can translate one person's speech to another					
Hears what is not said					
Interprets the organisation's speech					
Can translate the organisation's speech					

Total score out of 25=

Table 3.4   Get someone else to rate your skills as a Translator

	1 Awful	2 Poor	3 Adequate	4 Good	5 Superb
Hear what is really being said					
Can translate one person's speech to another					
Hears what is not said					
Interprets the organisation's speech					
Can translate the organisation's speech					

Total score out of 25=

CHAPTER 4

THE CULTIVATOR

THE SALES DIRECTOR

I once worked for a client where one of my particular areas of concern was the Sales Division. I loved this part of the company. They were fun and spirited. They had not been well trained, however, and one of the objectives of the new Sales Director and myself was to generally upskill the Sales Managers. We didn't have a plan to do this. We diagnosed what was needed next, carried that out, discussed what had happened and why and then went onto the next phase. It worked very well. The Sales Managers certainly improved their general level of skill and the organisation had a notably higher cadre of management. The Sales Director would always refer to 'growing' his people and took particular care to see each as individuals. He was a Cultivator. He was TENDING to people. The basic assumption of the Cultivator is that *an organisation is a human system* not an engineering system. The Cultivator is able to take time with things and people, when they have to.

CHANGE IS A GROWING PROCESS

In psychological reality, change does not come from *acting on* an organisation to *make it* a better shape. This happens only in business reality. On the contrary, change is more of a growing process – growing in the sense of bringing things to fruition. This is what the Sales Director did. Change is more a developmental process; one that occurs across time, like growing up, where the organisation can get stuck in places along the way. This contrasts with the meaning of change in business reality where it is seen as being able to race ahead. The Cultivator knows, metaphorically speaking, that one cannot go straight from being a child to being an adult without being an adolescent. One cannot force flowers to bloom. In short nothing can be done to force the next stage.

Pay Attention and Wait

The Cultivator knows it is not necessary to do anything, as such, to surface the next concern in a change process as the next stage is constantly emerging. This is comparable to the figure/ground dynamic that was shown in Chapter 2: The Seer. Psychological concerns present themselves. In psychological reality, you cannot always look for 'change accelerators'. One must instead learn that, at times, you pay attention and wait and then, later, you speed ahead. The accustomed notion we have of 'putting a change programme in place' belongs in business reality. To approach psychological reality like this renders it incomprehensible. You have to know how to wait and watch and when to wait and watch as well as when to put your foot on the accelerator. All of this is about pacing. John Kotter (2006, p. 240) states "the most general lesson to be learned is that the change process goes through a series of phases ... that, in total, usually require a considerable length of time". He cautions about skipping steps in this process.

PASSED OVER FOR PROMOTION

This is illustrated in the next story. I once had a client where a good manager had been passed over for a promotion. Everyone was upset about it, including the managers who had made the decision to pass him over. The passed-over manager was very distraught and I had decided to partly take him under my wing. His boss, who had made the infamous decision, was concerned to do the right thing so that the manager would get back to business as fast as possible. I was asked by him how long would it take for him to get over it. I said he, the senior manager, had to wait about six months before this manager was firing on all cylinders again. There was simply a process the relevant manager had to go through. The senior manager who asked me was aghast. He had wanted the process to take about two weeks. It didn't. I had counselled patience and, although the senior manager tried to have that patience, in the end he gave in to the impulse to push the manager concerned into another reasonable role. It didn't work. The manager struggled from then on for years, in fact, to function as well as he had done previously, and never got his sea legs. Eventually he got a secondment out of the company to a watchdog in the City of London.

LACK OF THE CULTIVATOR

In the same client as the Sales Director/ Cultivator existed another manager, the Business Director, who had none of the Cultivator. Much of my time was spent trying to get him to be one. He was always trying to get me to help him figure out who to fire. He wanted to go fast when he should go slow, and he was cautious and slow when he should have been like lightning. I met with him about every fortnight and we usually discussed what was happening from the point of view of the large scale change process we spearheaded. We made real progress when he stopped trying to stomp all over the company and stopped making progress when

I and others around him couldn't stop his bull headed ways. All of his mistakes came from a lack of the Cultivator.

Rhythm and Pace

In other words, the Cultivator knows that the rhythm and pace of time are different inside psychological reality rather than business reality. To assume that psychological reality moves steadily or stays the same throughout is linear thinking. This is consistent with business reality but inconsistent with psychological reality. In the latter, allowances need to be made for different speeds, paces and rhythms. Time is not linear: sometimes it is faster and sometimes much slower, Sometimes longstanding problems dissolve like magic and sometimes they don't. At these moments, it can seem that everything is in slow motion and you are anchored to the spot.

Assuming that the rhythm of events will vary is equivalent to allowing for a process of digestion to occur after eating. Programmed change sometimes results in corporate indigestion, not because the input is wrong but because there was no change of pace that allowed the company time to digest the input. The Cultivator knows that certain things grow and change at different speeds. They pace themselves and are able to gauge that in others.

THE CULTIVATOR

- Pace themselves and others
- Can be fast but ABLE to be slow
- Holds tension
- Act as Doctors (GPs)
- Understand different rhythms
- Able to give birth/ be creative
- Wellness assumptions

PRUNING COURSES

One thing that you would do as a Cultivator in any context is to prune things.

I once ran a course during which I decided that I needed to prune my business in order to grow it. (This is the Cultivator). In order to work out what to prune and what to leave, I sat on the side of the course while another presenter was teaching and got a piece of paper which I headed up with the following sections. The first section was headed 'Drop'. This would be the pile from which I would extract the pieces of work which needed to be pruned. For one reason or another, I loathed them. The second column of my piece of paper was headed 50/50, the third column was 'good' and the last, 'brilliant'.

I focused on which courses to drop. Unfortunately I had put the course I was currently teaching in that column, which had probably prompted me to do the exercise in the first place. After jotting my findings down, I went into the middle of the room to teach my session of that day's course.

As luck would have it, the client visited us that day and idly walked up to the table where I had left my notes describing the various courses I ran. I almost passed out as I pretended to not notice him fixated on reading my notes evaluating the various courses. He could hardly have failed to read the one relating to the current course.

He would have been quite within his rights to ask me "in that case, why are you teaching it?" That, however, was exactly why I had written the list – to extract myself from things I didn't want to do. I should have written or left the list somewhere else, though, not where anyone could see it. The essential point was that I had to actually drop those extra courses, not just put them on a wish list of what I 'wanted' to drop. Activating the Cultivator requires that you live it out. Pruning, for a Cultivator, is an essential part of a growth process.

ENGAGEMENT

I once did some research in a company I was working for. It was aimed at deciphering what creates high engagement rather than low engagement in employees. The top 20 and the bottom 40 were compared. The top performers were all Cultivators. They paced themselves and their employees. Most importantly, the top performers worked very hard but always had time for personal conversation. As a result the atmosphere was fun, open and honest. The employees didn't feel like objects but humans. The practices in the low performers were the opposite but they didn't have a clue why that was the case. They were much less personal and didn't want to be.

THE CULTIVATOR AS DOCTOR

Another name for the Cultivator is the Doctor, signifying a local GP rather than a specialist. My nickname in organisations has frequently been the 'Doctor', signifying the idea of getting a diagnosis and remedies. In one such company, they used that label to indicate that they would go to me with any 'complaint' and get some kind of diagnosis and prescription. I was a walking generalist with an emphasis on diagnosis. They even had a line in their budget for me called "Annamaria wandering around the company". I was allowed to book time with anyone about anything because they trusted that I would act in the organisation's interest.

The key purpose of the Cultivator/Doctor is to patiently diagnose the health and wellbeing of the organisation. Cultivators can monitor moods. These can reflect symptoms of well-being. The key skills are diagnosing, knowing the remedy. Knowing when to watch and when to act. Knowing about rhythms informs them to make wiser decisions.

The Process of Creatively Giving Birth

Cultivators also give birth to new things, or are responsible for others to 'give birth'; to orchestrate the process of giving birth. We often give birth to things in organisations, with a prior gestation process. Some people are quite good at this sort of thing, at creating new things. They are there to see the process occurs quite smoothly. Patience is vital during this process.

I was hired to work with the top managers of a large global company in the UK. The company was looking for their next generation of solutions. What is really going on here? The company is needing to give birth to a new company or new version of itself. Any pangs, therefore will be growing pains or birthing pains rather than standard resistance pains. The role most needed in this situation was the Cultivator, helping them bring forth. They were a scientific company. This process was designed to aid them coming up with the most creative solution.

The Cultivator Aids the Sick

Cultivators also aid an organisation that is sick and prescribe remedies. They perform operations, cut the organisation up and sew it up again, convincing people to stop moaning as these operations occur, or they will not be well again. The underlying model of this role is, therefore, a wellness one. They convince others that they will be well again, and that they are perfectly all right anyway.

You do not, however, want to see or have the need of a Cultivator all the time. If you do, you are likely to be sent to 'hospital' where they will examine you intensively. One of the basic assumptions is to see whether you imagine you will get well or that you will remain sick.

Will Schutz used to tell a tale of an Esalen-style series of workshops he ran. He ran them alongside a series of others, run by other workshop presenters. In a prior series, one participant had become very uncomfortable and left. He made a complaint, which was later conveyed to all the teachers. When it came time to the next series of workshops the teachers took different stances. One colleague decided to stress the availability to 'help', a counsellor down the corridor, so that every participant knew there was somewhere to go if needed. On that workshop, several people did avail themselves of this opportunity: Will took a different stance: he decided to not tell any of his next participants of this counsellor, nor that they could 'go down the corridor if feeling uncomfortable'. None of his participants did. What is going on here? His interpretation was that, if you assume wellness not potential ill-health you won't get any 'breakdown'. His stance stemmed from his general principle of 'Choice'; you can choose to be well or unwell. We make these choices all the time.

STAYING PRESENT WITH ANXIETY

The birthing process-creativity can only be successful by 'staying with' anxiety. Birthing processes and other creative processes occur regularly in organisations – whether the launch of a product, organisation, idea, new structure in the organisation.

But there is differential skill in how well these creative processes are managed. Some appropriate responses increase or maintain the level of anxiety present because that is the nature of what is occurring. These are the effective Cultivators: those who know when to increase anxiety, or allow the increase in anxiety, because that is inevitable in the process they are engaged in. Personally, they do not get bothered by it – it is all part of the game.

To a Cultivator, change is three dimensional. They know when to 'allow' anxiety and its manifestations. When and how to encourage people to hold their anxiety so that they do not endanger the birth or creation process. It cannot occur without some anxiety.

METAPHOR

You can use the Cultivator as a metaphor to understand what this role is about. If you were cultivating a garden what are the essential processes? If you were cultivating a group of people what would you do? Most of all, what would you do to cultivate yourself?

MODEL OF CHANGE FOR THE CULTIVATOR

I have already referred to the propensity of the Cultivator to 'stay with' anxiety, or manage it not suppress it. Some of the most interesting work done on anxiety is by Karen Horney, years ago. She discovered (Horney, 1945) three different kinds of reaction to anxiety, Moving Against People, Moving Towards People and Moving Away from People.

If handled correctly, which the Cultivator will, the functional responses to anxiety can move you along a change process. All three can be positive and stem from a basic assumption of wellness rather than illness.

Table 4.1   The effect of wellness assumptions

	Moving Against	Moving Towards	Moving Away
Illness assumptions	Aggression, belittling, manic	Overly social, burdensome	Retreats, runs away, not available
Wellness assumptions	Proactive, enduring, hardworking	Sociable, people gatherer	Creating space, independent

With the Cultivator present, anxiety is more likely to be channeled into the assumptions of wellness. It is not that common for these assumptions to be uppermost. Likewise, the Cultivator is not often present in organisations.

GETTING ANOTHER PERSPECTIVE: BOUNDARIES, CLOSURE AND SELF-INVESTMENT

As part of my PhD thesis I described in Chapter 3 (Garden, 1985), my underlying research question related to how to be *healthy*. This relates to the Cultivator because it is about health, about growing processes, about the Doctor healing. These findings were not explained by Jungian theory but by Gestalt theory.

These themes distinguished high-burnout from low-burnout groups:

- Boundaries
- Closure
- Self-investment

Boundaries

The Boundaries theme refers to the fact that those who scored high on burnout had weak permeable boundaries with the outside world and the low scorers on burnout had strong impermeable boundaries. The high group revealed a sense of immersion and losing of self. "I try to put so much into things I lose myself … I need to be as near to the vital element as possible". Unlike the high burnout group, the low group is characterized by a sense of experiencing a separateness between their work and their person. For the low group there is the notion of the subject running the object; the awareness that they are more important than their work.

Closure

The essence of this second theme can be considered to be diffusion over time as distinct from diffusion over space of the boundaries theme. In this theme, the 'high' group exhibit difficulties experiencing closure, or finishing something. At the same time they exhibit a compulsive need to finish something. The low group, on the other hand, experience closure more easily, find it easy to let go of things and do not exhibit the same compulsion to finish what they begin.

Self-Investment

This third theme focuses on the stance an individual takes to the world in terms of the investment of self that takes place. The high group emphasizes the self-investment side with little appraisal of the return. The low group emphasizes the return, or self-interest, side of the exchange. The differences relate to being effort-oriented or outcome-oriented. In the former, the individual stance is one of what is put into something compared with a stance of what can be got out of something. What satisfies the high group is a sense that they have given as much as they could, that their self-contribution has been maximized. The low group takes a different stance. This group is concerned with what is taken and make very deliberate calculations to ensure that any input of effort will be worth it in terms of expected output. Their satisfaction derives not from having "given their all" but from getting the most out of as little effort as necessary.

What Does it Mean for the Cultivator?

One of the overarching themes is the importance of pacing and rhythm (Cultivator). The low burnout group is able to pace themselves at their pace. The high burnout group is demonstrating what Gestalt therapy would call an 'introject'. In other words, they have absorbed wholesale an idea or admonition, when they were younger. It is someone else's idea, not their's so they have taken it in, without 'chewing it'. This is what is driving their unproductive self-harming behaviour. It is the Cultivator role which would notice this behaviour and, be able to do something about it.

OD TOOLS TO LEAVE WITH CULTIVATORS

Books: Nevis, E. 2001; Horney. K. 1945; Mann. D. 2010; Polster E and M. 1974; Kotter, J. 2002.

John Kotter's Theory of Change

One major contribution to the Cultivator's ways of doing things is John Kotter's theory of change. He has studied change in hundreds of companies. He describes "the most general lesson to be learned from the more successful cases is that the change process goes through a series of phases that, in total, usually require a considerable length of time. Skipping steps creates only the illusion of speed and never produces a satisfying result. A second very general lesson is that critical mistakes in any of the phases can have a devastating impact, slowing momentum and negating hard-won wins" (Kotter, 2006, p. 240). There are eight steps to change in his model, set in a context of See-Feel-Change rather than Analysis-Think-Change

- Establishing a sense of urgency
- Forming a powerful guiding coalition
- Creating a vision
- Communicating the vision
- Empowering others to act on the vision
- Planning for and creating short-terms wins
- Consolidating improvements and producing still more change
- Institutionalizing new approaches (adapted from Kotter, 2006, p. 243)

Gestalt Psychology and Ed Nevis

The term Gestalt comes from the idea of completion and 'a whole'. A 'gestalt', therefore is the completion of a need in a person. When it is completed there is a whole experience. Similarly, when it is completed, i.e., when the need is met, the gestalt is completed and the person can move on to other needs and seek a gestalt, or completion with them. When people refer to needing 'closure' they are saying they want a whole experience or a gestalt. Until that closure happens they cannot allow new needs to surface in order to gain fulfilment.

One of the major figures in Gestalt (therapy) is Ed Nevis, who was a Professor at MIT when I was there. He and his wife helped me with my dissertation on burnout pointing out the Gestalt implications of my findings. Sonya was the one who pointed out the idea of an introject being part of the equation.

One of the things Gestalt is characterized by is The Cycle, or The Cycle of Experience. "The Cycle summarises the process by which people ... become aware of what is going on at any moment, and how they mobilise energy to take some action that allows them to deal constructively with possibilities suggested by the new awareness". (Nevis, 2001, p. 1). Closure occurs in this cycle when the person either learns or gets some meaning from the whole cycle that has just happened. Note that the whole cycle of experience is structured around there being different phases, of a different character or nature.

One of Ed Nevis's particular contributions is the distinction between different modes of influence. He refers to them as provocative and evocative. Both are useful in their own way for different situations and needs. Ed's book is one of the classic OD books written from a Gestalt perspective.

Kurt Lewin: Force Field Analysis

Force Field Analysis is partly a tool for Navigators but also for Cultivators. It is a way of mapping forces for a change, balanced by forces against a change. The language being spoken in is that of pressures and tension and forces. The solution to the analysis is clarity about what forces to increase and what to decrease. One of the secrets to this working, told to me by Dick Beckhard, is that the current situation is described by a balance of the forces against and those for, but when you try to get movement you need to decrease the forces against first. If you try to increase the forces for the change you will simply activate the commensurate amount of forces against. Reality is described by this tension between opposites. I have seen many people try this activity without understanding that important qualification.

20 QUESTIONS

Who are the Cultivators in your organisation?...

....

When have you been a Cultivator?..

....

What does it require?..

....

What response in others does it generate?..

....

Is your organisation in hospital?..

....

Does your organisation get well quickly or slowly?.............................

....

Does your organisation imagine it is usually well or unwell?...............

....

How easily does your organisation give birth to new things?...............

....

Who, in your organisation, is best at doing this?...................................

....

Can you recognize a gestation period?..

....

What is given birth to most easily?..

....

Do you make accurate diagnoses of what is going on in the organisation?............

....

How can you do your job/studies more as a Cultivator/Doctor?............................

....

Are the remedies you are currently applying the right ones?................................

....

Do you participate in birth processes in the organisation?...................................

....

If not, do you cut these off because of the tension or anxiety present?...................

....

Can you improve your response to the gestation period?......................................

....

Do you understand the anxiety responses around you?...

....

If not, what can you do to improve?...

....

If so, how can you make sure you keep those responses around?...........................

....

EXERCISES

The following section gives you some exercises to practice to be a Cultivator. You can do them as an employee, manager, student or as an OD consultant:

- **Exercise One**: Get together with a group you are working with in your organisation (or a student in class); together you are going to make a diagnosis of your organisation/ university. What extra tools can you use to do this diagnosis if you concentrate on the idea that you are all Cultivators. Limit yourself to diagnosis only NOT the remedies. Note that whenever you do a diagnosis in OD, do only that.
- **Exercise Two**: This exercise is an extension of the one above. Get together with a group you are working with in your organisation (or a student in class/a group); together you are going to work out remedies for your organisation/ university.
- **Exercise Three**: The main learning in this chapter is on pacing. Write yourself a minute-by-minute diary for one week. In it, put down your estimate of your pacing. Relate that pacing to the on-going requirements on you. Are you too static in your pacing?? Do you respond appropriately to your requirements? Are you, in general, too fast, too slow or about right?
- **Exercise Four**: Recall a creative task you should have done or should be doing. The next time you get the impulse to do something about it, start the creative task. You may well feel anxiety as you do this. Monitor yourself closely: is your anxiety manifesting itself in terms of you wanting to Go towards people, Go away from people or Go against people? That is your anxiety response. Stay WITH that anxiety and keep going with the creative task. Don't give into the anxiety.
- **Exercise Five**: Imagine your organisation is ill. It is exhausted. What has happened to it that would create this exhaustion. Imagine the culture of your organisation. Does it have proper boundaries, a proper sense of closure and a proper attention to managing its time and energy? (Think in terms of the burnout research). How can you create wellness assumptions for the organisation? How can you create remedies?

Table 4.2   Rate your own skill as a Cultivator

	1 Awful	2 Poor	3 Adequate	4 Good	5 Superb
Able to pace yourself					
Able to hold anxiety					
Know how to create birth					
Understand changing rhythms					
Assume wellness					

Total score out of 25=

Table 4.3   Rate your colleagues or team as Cultivators

	1 Awful	2 Poor	3 Adequate	4 Good	5 Superb
Able to pace yourself					
Able to hold anxiety					
Know how to create birth					
Understand changing rhythms					
Assume wellness					

Total score out of 25=

Table 4.4   Get someone else to rate your skills as a Cultivator

	1 Awful	2 Poor	3 Adequate	4 Good	5 Superb
Able to pace yourself					
Able to hold anxiety					
Know how to create birth					
Understand changing rhythms					
Assume wellness					

Total score out of 25=

CHAPTER 5

THE CATALYST

FOLLOWING THE INTENT

In one consulting assignment in the UK the task was to get the top 200 managers to chart their way into the future. They were asked in the workshops to work out strategic and organisational breakthroughs for the company, partly by knowing the terrain they were currently in more acutely than before. We succeeded Gary Hamel and C.K. Prahalad, whose mission working with this company had been along the lines of determining their strategic intent.

Implementing Strategy Faster

Our programme was about "implementing strategy faster", a slogan they had worked out for themselves on the prior programme run by Gary and C.K. The company had roughed out their strategy to a great extent with them, but they knew they were weak at implementation. They knew they were weak at 'people' and 'culture'.

Our own programme involved three presenters. We had the top 200 managers through a series of one week workshops with, usually, three management teams on each. This was a device used to get interaction across the company and cross pollination of ideas.

The programmes were to get the intact work team, consisting of a manager and his/her group, to determine a series of actions and strategies that would meet the overall aim. After a few workshops for these top 200 managers, the main thrust in the company was to furiously tear away at the bureaucracy. While that was going on, others were creating skunkworks and new organisations. One group had started to create a range of computers in different colours and other groups were starting to invent completely new products.

Most of these actions stemmed from the actions of one set of people and a series of interactions we had with them. There was a domino effect happening. The OD question is: what made this original group set out on their enterprising way and revolutionise the company?

CHANGING THE COMPANY

The origin of this behaviour was on one of the first workshops. One of the teams was the Finance team, led by the Chief Accountant (who almost ran the company) and his team of accountants and a Business Director. On the five day programme they were taken through a staged set of exercises to discuss the strategy, along with a focus on implementing strategy faster. One of the general issues and gripes in the company was its extreme bureaucracy.

The three teams each had to prepare a way forward for their group and for the company and prepare a presentation at which the MD would be present, on Friday. In their break out group, the Finance team had gone great guns. Partly stimulated by one of the junior accountants, they had worked out a vision of a company that was entrepreneurial and free of bureaucracy. The key to implementing this vision was their own area, Finance. Unless they relaxed the myriad of controls and financial strangulation, the company could never become as nimble as it needed to be. They worked out what, few, controls, they would need. We were delighted with their intentions and they were pleased as punch with themselves.

On Friday, the team had to present their ideas to the other two intact work teams to get their reaction and feedback. The MD was not going to be present after all. The Chief Accountant did the presentation. They had gone back on all their new ideas; and focused on the need for control and presented a formula for bureaucracy. I was fuming and interrupted them, challenging them over their boring bureaucratic vision of the company. They shut up and sat down. They refused to speak to me, which was fine, and joined up again as a group during a coffee break and rapidly put together again their entrepreneurial plan. They came back and presented that new plan to the whole group, to great acclaim but still not talking to me.

Their team did, in fact, implement their new plan, just as they said, and many of the old financial controls and measures were jettisoned. The company changed extensively and rapidly as I described earlier. This team and their actions were just the Catalyst the company needed.

Fast Change from a Catalyst

Fast change like this will only ever come from the actions of a Catalyst. Long-drawn out change, which is what usually occurs, arises because no one has had the nous or the courage to act as a Catalyst. Being a Catalyst requires going out on a limb. In this case we had the junior accountant followed by the Chief Accountant both acting as Catalysts.

I DO NOT NEED THIS CONTRACT

The most impactful piece of consulting advice Dick Beckhard ever gave me was that, each time you walk through the door of a client, you say to yourself that 'I do not need this client'. Needless to say, you have to really mean it. This means that when you are working with them or meeting with them, you put yourself out on a limb, you are creative and take risks.

Dick Beckhard was the stroppiest Catalyst I have ever met. Some people don't think that is OD. They prefer people in OD to soft pedal; to soft-shoe shuffle. In my view if you can't be a Catalyst and confront then you are not an OD person.

HITTING THE BULLSEYE

How do they have this effect? Because they know how to hit the bullseye. Because of this they are transformers and dramatic. They usually work at a more than usually rapid pace. This is in complete contrast to the Cultivator. If you are moving fast and *still in touch with psychological reality*, you know you are being a Catalyst. Their effects are all-encompassing, stemming from the fact that their client is the organisation not an individual. The effects of the Catalyst are that something happened as if by magic. Some managers have the effect of altering a wide range of things, and people, in a flash. They have a magical key. They can only do this by taking risks; including risks with themselves. They have to be reasonably self-aware to take risks with themselves. I watched Dick Beckhard with several clients and he was always a Catalyst; he would follow the client's speech, listening acutely, and after a while he would hit upon the answer (or question). It always meant taking a risk; exposing himself because the idea was always out of left field. Usually he would preface what he was going to say with "I am going to suggest something stupid" and then present his idea. It always worked. The client would say "that's it". It was always a breakthrough. Dick refers to himself in his autobiography as a Catalyst (Beckhard, 1997, p. 22).

Slippery Data

One of the difficulties of being a Catalyst is that you are working with very slippery data; with feelings and hunches and barely perceptible thoughts. But you get used to this vague collection of data and trust it once you start working in a catalytic way.

The key purpose of the Catalyst is to know how, when and in what way to transform the organisation. One key element is that they enlighten, bring light on things. By doing this they create something new out of the old. The Catalyst transforms.

TAKING RISKS

One ingredient of the Catalyst is to take risks which means to "leave your ego at the front door" as Dick Beckhard would have said. I once ran a programme with a large struggling retail company in the UK; a household name that was trying to stay afloat. They had just been bought out by a consortium, known to the City of London, and so they had a bit of a breather within which they could try to demonstrate they could turn the company around. The managers were untrained and highly resistant to any change. We ran a five-day programme for all the top managers. Then we got down to business and taught them some basics of management, including MBTI™, Firo-B, for example. We intervened throughout to get them onto the same wavelength as the new senior managers. One group was the most resistant of the lot. I knew that some of these managers might be made redundant, and that they were playing with their jobs by not getting their minds around what was going on in the company. So, at a certain point, when I was up the front, I stopped and confronted them with what they were doing. I said they needed to be focused on "spreading their wings" (in the 'new' company) but all they were doing was moaning about everything that was happening. I told them that I was going off to get a cup of coffee downstairs and when they had decided they would spread their wings, they could come and get me and I would start teaching again.

I then walked downstairs and sat with a coffee until they came to get me. I wasn't absolutely sure that they would come and get me, but all I knew was that we were getting nowhere fast unless they altered their approach. I was a bit on edge but sat there.

Eventually, someone came to get me saying, they were going to spread their wings now. I went back up, very relieved and we got on with what we were supposed to be doing. They started to do things that were, to them, radically new. Apart from anything else, they did in fact salvage their jobs.

THE CATALYST

- Hits the bulls eye
- Ignores the contract
- Takes risks
- Carries excitement
- Can move at speed
- Leaves ego at front door
- Handles slippery data

ABSENCE OF CATALYSTS

I once worked with a Government Department in the UK. The course was held at Cranfield School of Management, where I had done my MBA, near Bedford. It was a five day programme and on the Wednesday, we always had a bit of a break. During a three hour period, the managers had to go outside the School and find a way to discover what motivates people in their job. Needless to say we expected them to find some employees somewhere and ask them or watch them at work and answer the puzzle posed. Every group of managers loved this exercise. Except the Government Department. Before the groups disappeared outside, they were expected to plan for 20–30 mins. The best groups were always those who were so eager that they tore out the door and planned in the car driving somewhere. The government department sat on the couches talking. And talking and talking and talking. They planned everything down to the most minute detail. Then they decided not to go because they already knew the answer. They already knew what motivates people. I kicked them out the door about one and a half hours after the start point. What was occurring was a complete absence of any spark, any Catalyst. They lived in a comfort zone where they dwelled in a slew of satisfaction and no excitement.

A CATALYST CAN BE CREATED (WITH THE RIGHT CONDITIONS)

A Catalyst might seem to be innately personal. Yet I have seen Catalysts created out of thin air. We can see this in the design for a workshop that followed on from the workshop I have already described in the beginning of this chapter where I was focused on 'Implementing strategy faster'.

After a year and a bit, every top team had been through the first workshop. They wanted more and we were asked to carry on and draw up a design that would meet their further needs. This would be called Mark II. They wanted voluntary participation. They wanted a workshop structure that was more in-depth, focused within one division or area of business present. They wanted plans and focus.

So we designed a workshop that rested on having present some of the 'troops', that is, the people at the coal face like salespeople, engineers or people two or three levels below the management team. In addition we did a form of 360 degree feedback with respondents including the sales teams, customers, suppliers, members of the Manexec, other divisions and their own division. But, the more important catalyst was the presence of the troops with the most senior managers in the company.

The workshops began with feeding back the massive 360 degree feedback. It was essential to do this in a company like their's because they were tough hard-bitten managers. They were high on camaraderie but, to get through to them on an issue, meant a combination of beating their heads in and selling them an idea.

The engine room were the key intervention of the workshop. They were the stars. They were always a bit scared (what if they lost their jobs telling the top managers what to do with the company). I always separated the two groups initially, to address 3 questions. The focus of each set was aimed at telling their counterpoint group what they wanted them to do differently to what they were doing. For the engine room, they were asked to say how they would run the company, where would they make savings if they were running the company, and what were the sacred cows in the company. The bosses were asked what they would want the engine room to do more of, less of, and so on.

The critical ingredient to 'create Catalysts' was to slowly but surely get them to drop their egos in favour of functioning solely in the interests of the organisation. They were asked to be creative. The atmosphere was always light hearted and fun. Next, they had to tell it like it is. Every time, without exception, when I ran 'engine room' sessions, the effect was electrifying. This is the Catalyst at work.

In one workshop, the engine room highlighted that the sacred cows, savings to be made, were the same: that they didn't care about having company cars in the way the senior managers thought they did and they didn't need offices. The senior managers didn't believe them at first but the engine room was insistent. Soon, some of the offices were closed and they sold half the cars.

MODEL OF CHANGE FOR CATALYSTS

My model of change for Catalysts is developing what is called a 'transcendent function' as per the psychologist, Carl Jung, (Jung, 1960; 1966; 1971; see Appendix 2 which sets out my elaboration partly as it relates to the transcendent function).

In developing this transcendent function, there results high energy, a new situation, it is dynamic. The outcome is marvelous. How does it arise? By taking risks and *combining radically different things*.

What is a transcendent function? It is a term used by Carl Jung but not often referred to in relation to the MBTI™. I take a more Jungian approach. One aspect of that is to be wary of always talking only of a type, such as ENTP or INFP. Nor should one focus on developing one's MBTI™ type in accordance with what is externally appropriate. What I focus on, as a Catalyst, is what is appropriate *internally*. If you do the latter then pretty soon you will be wondering about the 'transcendent function'. The change that occurs with the latter is akin to the functioning of a Catalyst.

"This is … the more important part of the procedure, the bringing together of opposites for the production of a third: the transcendent function". (Jung, 1960, p. 87). The 'bringing together of opposites' referred to by Jung means that one has reasonably developed, say, the sensing function and also reasonably developed your intuitive function (these two functions being theoretically opposites). The other two functions that are theoretically opposites are the thinking and feeling function. However, there is also a natural bent, called 'individuation' that brings the psyche to create a Transcendent function. "Balancing the two [thinking and feeling, for example] is what creates the transcendent function" (Jung, 1960, p. 87).

"The confrontation of the two positions [e.g., thinking and feeling] generates a tension charged with energy and creates a living birth that leads to a new level of being, a new situation. The transcendent function manifests as a quality of conjoined opposites" (Jung, 1960, p. 90.) In other words, it is a drive of the Self of each of us that tries to push us to be psychic Catalysts and unite separate single functions.

GETTING ANOTHER PERSPECTIVE: JOB EXCITEMENT AND JOB SATISFACTION

I once did some unpublished research on the differences between job excitement and job satisfaction. I was researching the small rapid growth high tech companies primarily in Cambridge, UK. The Catalysts live in the world of excitement rather than satisfaction. While the Cultivators manage anxiety and can be quite comfortable with it, the Catalyst manages excitement and can be quite comfortable with it.

In my study, I divided the research sample up into different size organisations, from under 50 people in 7 companies, between 150–250 people in 3 companies, to over 2000 people in 1 company. They were a good 'knowledge' worker sample as 96 per cent had degrees.

The feeling of 'excitement should be distinguished from a feeling of 'satisfaction'. Satisfaction refers to a need being fulfilled. It is a low tension state, allied with contentment. The key distinguishing characteristic of these two states is the degree of alertness and energy contained in them. The distinction is an important one. The task of satisfying employees may be different from the task of keeping them excited. In other words, the spirit of excitement in an organisation is not obtained through people being satisfied. In practice, however, managers who are concerned with keeping the energy of the small company alive, talk in terms of keeping their employees happy and satisfied not in terms of keeping them alert and on-the-go.

Increasing Satisfaction with Size

The results indicated exactly what you might imagine. Levels of excitement decreased the larger the company and levels of satisfaction increased with size of organisation.

Different job and organisational factors were associated with the feelings of job excitement and satisfaction.

The factors associated with job excitement are not identical to those associated with job satisfaction. The satisfaction items can be seen as 'hygiene' factors. These reflect resources and perks, things the company can give to the employee. They have an overall sense of the employee being provided for, given to, looked after.

The variables associated with job excitement are very different and reflect the individual being fully used and feeling useful. They are to do with feeling stretched and with feeling that their inner resources, their talents and skills are being used. These variables involve a sense of wanting to contribute to the company rather than wanting the company to contribute to them. To give rather than to be given to.

What was also interesting was to examine what happened to these factors as the organisation got bigger. The levels of those variables previously chosen to be associated with job excitement decrease with organisational size. The presence of the satisfaction factors increase. In other words, those key factors most associated with job excitement are less in evidence in the large company compared with the medium and, in turn, the small companies.

What is the lesson? Probably the aim is to achieve both job excitement and job satisfaction.

OD TOOLS TO LEAVE WITH CATALYSTS

Books: Beckhard, R. 1997; Beckhard. R. and Pritchard, W. 1992; Beckhard, R. 1969; Bailyn, L. 2006; Goffee R. and Jones, G. 1988.

Dick Beckhard's Confrontation meeting

A confrontation meeting involves different levels in the organisation in a meeting that either resolves key organisational differences, or sets up some strategic guidance for the senior managers (partly by involving the troops who may not be listened to that often). The context is improving the health of the organisation. As Dick states, one "of the continuing problems facing the top management team of any organization in times of stress or major change is knowing how to assess accurately the state of the organization's health. How are people reacting to the change? How committed are subordinate managers to the new conditions? Where are the most pressing organization problems?" (Beckhard, 1997, p. 177).

At these times senior managers often work intensively together. Even while they often become more cohesive they become more cut-off from middle managers and the troops. Communications become worse and people feel left out.

Dick formulated an activity "that allows a total management group, drawn from all levels of the organization, to take a quick reading of its own health and –within a matter of hours-to set action plans for improving it. I call this activity a confrontation meeting" (Beckhard, 1997, p. 178).

This speed is symptomatic of the Catalyst as is drawing different strands of people together. The confrontation meeting is an activity that is done in a short space of time, given the amount of inputs and outputs involved. People need to be committed to the process.

The steps taken are:

- Climate setting: it is important to establish everyone's commitment to the process
- Information collection: getting all feelings and opinions out in the open
- Information sharing: making sure all the information for the confrontation meeting is shared
- Priority setting: people break into work-unit groups and set priorities
- Organisation action planning: getting commitment from senior managers for the action plans
- Immediate follow-up by top team: senior managers plan their commitments
- Progress review: monitoring the process as it unfolds

Dick calls this intervention a 'micromechanism' and credits it with providing the total management group with "an accurate reading of the organization's health" (Beckhard, 1997, p. 188).

Lotte Bailyn's 'Breaking the Mold'

In Breaking the Mold, Lotte's concern is with the separation of work and family which she argues is no longer a viable option for employees or organisations. "But the underlying assumption of separate work and personal domains persists" (Bailyn, 2006, p. xi). It is essential in today's business world that they are integrated, and this brings benefits to employees and their employers. "It is the thesis of this book ... that framing the issue as a conflict between employees' private needs and the competitive and productivity needs of US enterprise is self-defeating for both.

I hope to provide a different way of thinking about the link between public and private life that will allow the work of US companies to be organized to create synergy rather than conflict between the two spheres. The goal is to break the mold of traditional assumptions: the hope is that the needs of organizations and employees can be brought into constructive harmony" (Bailyn, 2006, p. 4). This is a Catalyst in both manner of speech is well as substantive content. Referring to the aim as 'breaking the mold' reminds you of the confrontation that is naturally a Catalyst. Similarly, the objective of the research is huge: changing the way of integrating public and private life. The central argument is that if employees' needs were catered for, companies would themselves become more productive.

For that to happen, employers need to challenge some of their basic assumptions about what work is, as well as time, commitment and career success. I have classified this as a Catalyst tool because of the fact that she, and her colleagues distinguish between work and family not as needing to be in 'balance', but rather than needing to be *integrated*. They reject the former approach and argue for integration. This means two different things (the Catalyst) come together and a third is created (the integration).

Goffee and Jones: The Character of the Corporation

Goffee and Jones use two sociological concepts – solidarity and sociability – to create a framework that integrates them. They construct a theory of different cultures: networked, fragmented, communal, mercenary are the basic types of culture. These can appear in positive or negative form. Any one organisation can be any mix of these. They state "it's fair to say that for the last twenty years we have been struggling to understand the kinds of social relationships within organisations that help them cohere and make them successful" (1998, p. ix). In other words, they are not interested in defining culture per se, but of delineating different ways of the culture working for not against the company.

20 QUESTIONS

Who in your organisation acts as a Catalyst?..

....

When have you had the effect of being a Catalyst?...

....

What behaviour was required?...

....

What response does it generate?..

....

Do you have the courage necessary to be a Catalyst?...

....

What conditions were relevant in the organisation at the time
this occurred?...

....

Are you ready to make sudden shifts in the organisation?...................................

....

Are you, in general, the 'spark' in your organisation?...

....

How might you start to create a sea-change?...

....

Do people in your organisation take risks?..

....

Do they take risks with themselves?...

....

Are the people who provide a spark, acknowledged?..

....

Are people in your organisation easily able to confront issues...............................

....

Can you confront and have a constructive effect?..

....

Are there people in your organisation who 'hit the bullseye?'................................

....

Do you occasionally have effects disproportionate to your actions?......................

....

Is your organisation a Catalyst in your environment?..

....

Can your organisation operate at great speed?...

....

Can your organisation can change at great speed?...

....

Can you operate at great speed?...

....

EXERCISES

The following section gives you some exercises to practice to be a Catalyst. You can do them as an employee, or manager, student or as an OD consultant.

- **Exercise One**: Imagine you are approaching a new client (manager). As you get towards her/him say to yourself "I do not need this contract (job)". Now greet them. How do you feel?
- **Exercise Two**: Do you know 1–2 Catalysts in your organisation/client? What are they like? Are they likeable? What do they do that is different than what you do?
- **Exercise Three**: Are you good at taking risks? If so, you are an actual or latent Catalyst. How could you help others be more catalytic? If not, you need to practice more risks if you want to be a Catalyst.
- **Exercise Four**: Is your organisation/ client creating too much satisfaction and not enough excitement? Put another way, does your organisation/client use satisfaction variables at the expense of excitement factors? If so, put on the agenda the variables that create excitement.
- **Exercise Five**: Think whether you have developed two of the related Jungian/MBTI™ functions. In other words, have you developed a reasonable thinking function as well as a reasonable feeling function. The next step in your development is to not leave them like that but to develop a 'transcendent' function, as per Jung. This consists of an integration of the two developed functions, creating a third function. Think about how you might do this. It will be your own personal change mirroring change in the organisation.

Table 5.1   Rate your own skill as a Catalyst

	1 Awful	2 Poor	3 Adequate	4 Good	5 Superb
I take risks with myself					
I am a spark					
I transform things					
I easily carry excitement					
My interventions are electrifying					

Total score out of 25=

Table 5.2   Rate your colleagues or team as Catalysts

	1 Awful	2 Poor	3 Adequate	4 Good	5 Superb
I take risks with myself					
I am a spark					
I transform things					
I easily carry excitement					
My interventions are electrifying					

Total score out of 25=

Table 5.3   Get someone else to rate your skills as a Catalyst

	1 Awful	2 Poor	3 Adequate	4 Good	5 Superb
I take risks with myself					
I am a spark					
I transform things					
I easily carry excitement					
My interventions are electrifying					

Total score out of 25=

CHAPTER 6

THE NAVIGATOR

BUYING A SECOND HAND PLANE AND FLYING ACROSS THE WORLD

My father flew an open-cockpit plane from England to Australia back in the 30's. As such, he was the pilot and co-pilot in one, and the functions of the navigator he had to absorb while flying the plane. He bought the plane second hand from Sir Gordon Selfridge, son of the owner of Selfridges in Oxford Street in London and had exchanged his second hand car for it. There was no radar in those days, for flights like his, and no radio contact, but he had one hand-held compass to show him where the directions north, south, east and west were. Any geographical maps he needed he copied out by hand at the local library, because his funds for the trip were so short.

In other words, there were few of the systems we now regard as necessary for flying. What he did to navigate was hang his head out the side to spot the nearest railway line, and follow it, as well as to 'use his nut' as he used to say. He could spot major landmarks, such as larger cities, or towns where he was supposed to get some fuel, from looking over the side ('windows') and from studying the hand-drawn maps he had. He would know which sea was below him, and so on, from these methods of navigation; looking at the hand-drawn maps, using his compass and looking over the side. He had these methods too to aid him in getting across the stretches of sea that existed between England and Australia. He simply kept flying till the sun went down. He made it safely in about 30 days, with a few adventures and scrapes. Now, that is a navigator. There is no way he could have survived except by good navigating and using his nut.

In companies, navigation is a little like this at least some of the time. If you can't do it, or the equivalent, you need to know someone who does. They do exist because I have met them. They are excellent 'guides' as to what is going on in the organisation and where the organisation is going. They listen to a word here and an action there and make two and two make an accurate rendition of the space they are currently in as well as the future path they need to take. Both OD people as well as managers can make great, inspirational Navigators.

Getting Round the System

My father, flying his small gypsy moth to Australia, had only just received his pilot's licence allowing him to fly, and had practiced about an extra 10 hours above that amount. He had, therefore, a total of only 40 hours before he set off from Croydon, England, on his big adventure. The main reason he wanted to do this journey was to add to his hours and get his commercial pilot's licence, and found flying to Australia infinitely more attractive than flying up and down the country merely adding up hours. However, in spite of his very good reason to gain his commercial pilots licence in this manner, the authorities didn't think it was a sensible idea. So he had to outwit them, which he did by flying out of Croydon airport, rather than a larger one, at some odd hour with only one person there at the airport to see him off. He had given them the slip. They had seen his trip as 'crazy', imagining he would not survive, particularly the last leg across the Baring strait (with all its sharks). Navigators often seem to be making 'crazy' journeys and, yet, they have very good reasons for doing what they are so earnestly set on doing. Sometimes they have to buck conventional wisdom to succeed in navigating well. It is an idiosyncratic role for an OD person or manager.

NAVIGATING IN ORGANISATIONS

The story illustrates some of the basic tenets of what is important to know about navigating in organisations. Even in my most sophisticated clients, especially if they are blue-skying, you may need to be able to do the equivalent of flying from England to Australia with no fancy radar or messages from a radio telling you whether or not you are off-course. You look out for the nearest railway line, river, tree or tall building to tell you instead. For example, a good navigator will be able to tell you which piece of the myriad data people pour through, is useful. They will ignore the rest. They prioritise information and have the courage to ignore data that isn't useful for navigation purposes. OD people do this kind of information gathering the whole time.

Another vital component of the Navigator is the ability to scan (as in a radar scanner). They walk in to a room and immediately have everyone and everything 'scanned'. They don't look at one particular person but know everything at a glance.

Artists Studios

But, it is more than just information gathering. I worked in one large manufacturing company and, along with faculty from London Business School, created a series of workshops that would allow them to create blue-sky solutions and set some sort of direction for the company. They weren't interested in setting goals as such yet. How should we, the consultants, deal with this? One example of what we did was to put them in artists' open studios with virtually no equipment but bare walls. We were following the same principle as 'flying anyway', without the basic equipment. Did we expect more creative solutions by giving them four bare walls rather than fancy luxury? Yes, we did. Is this a bit like going to the local library to create hand-drawn maps rather than buying them? Yes. Did it seem crazy? It did. It seemed crazy to the company but they relented anyway. They knew they were 'up against it'. All of it (readings, exercises, work) involved flying around in uncharted territory without a radio or radar screen to tell anyone where we were.

CHARTING A WAY THROUGH PSYCHOLOGICAL SPACE

To understand this role at a more conceptual level, a useful definition to get us started would be: 'navigating is about moving through uncharted territory. You may or may not have a compass. Even if you do have one it may provide you with the bare necessities'. Sometimes people use quantitative information as if it was a reliable compass reading simply because it is quantitative. However, that information can lead you to the wrong decisions because these numbers are only a guide. What if the numbers are wrong, misleading, a temporary blip. You need 'independence of thought' as the same time as analytical skills. If my father had been offered all the modern paraphernalia to fly down in his tiny plane, he would have taken them. But, he knew how to fly without them as well. This is when you need the skills of the navigator.

BLIND FLYING

My airborne father had a very interesting tale he used to tell about 'blind flying'. After he had made his trip flying to Australia, and then went to NZ barnstorming, he went back to a new flying school in Hove, UK, to "learn how to fly properly" as he put it. He wanted, 'especially' to "learn how to loop the loop" (somersaulting in the plane) because so many of his paying customers in NZ had asked him to do it and he couldn't. So off he went to flying school. One test they gave him was called 'blind flying'. He had to fly in a perfect triangle around Hove. All he was allowed to use was the instrument panel. The instructor was in the adjacent seat judging him. He recalls this as the worst moment of his life. Nevertheless he carved out a near perfect triangle such that his instructor said he was more accurate blind flying than looking out the window as normal. He won the trophy for they flight and kept it on our family mantelpiece for years.

What does it mean for a psychological Navigator? It means several things. To keep learning 'how to fly' and how to navigate. To fly without normal sight. To me it means being tested on using quantitative and qualitative data and how we should be able to use both.

A PSYCHOLOGICAL READING

To look at the Navigator dynamically, we need two things: we need the idea of figure and ground that was introduced in Chapter 2, The Seer (which is what Navigators pay attention to) and then examine the Navigator's model of change.

Within the frame of figure/ground, we need to be able to pay attention to events in a way that maps trends and movement. In other words we need to think dynamically. This will occur when the figure and ground relationship shifts and one psychological aspect recedes while another moves to the foreground.

An OD Navigator serves as both the radar screen for, and the guide through, unfamiliar territory. They do this in both psychological reality and business reality. Beckhard and Pritchard (1992, p. 1) state "competitive strategy will be a function of [having] maximum control over its own destiny". In contrast the Navigator role is about being able to navigate the rapids, a very different concept than maximum control.

The main thing the Navigator knows is that the particular psychological concern which is at the foreground at the moment must be resolved before it will fade back and become background. Unlike business reality, we cannot shuffle the priorities around and say "we don't have time to deal with this now. There are more important things to do". If we proceed like this, we inevitably will get tripped up by the fact that some priorities have a mind of their own. If our attention skips a concern or avoids one, it nevertheless will, in psychic space, remain figure. Eventually the anchor that is in the psychological realm will become a frustrating millstone weighing down progress. Unseen but definitely felt. Thus the key contribution of the navigator is to *chart a way through psychological space*.

The Lone Navigator

I once worked for an MD who was a Navigator. No one else in his executive committee was. He was forever doodling with envelopes drawing the direction of the company and the alternatives for getting to where he wanted to go. He definitely had 'independence of thought' and could have an independent opinion about anything including what was going on in the company and where it was going. He could conceptualise where the company might go quite easily whereas the others could not. There were numerous bust ups in the company but, under his direction, it sorted out what where they wanted to go, quite independent of what anyone in their industry was doing. This was the MDs influence.

NAVIGATING AS A METAPHOR

Often, we use this term in the context of navigating a car. A navigator sitting in a car might or might not be the driver. They may function as a navigator from the passenger seat as well as the driver seat.

When do you need a navigator? Often, the role is useful when people are driving somewhere but are unsure of the route or territory. You find 'navigators' emerging when the people involved want to go particularly fast. Or, when the road conditions are difficult for some reason, such as having a great many cars on the road, a navigator can free up the driver from looking at a map when they are supposed to be watching passing cars or the road.

You do, in fact, get navigators of machines other than cars. An aircraft has a pilot and a co-pilot, with one person primarily responsible for navigation while the other person flies the plane or is primarily responsible for doing so. A ship has navigators. So do companies.

A navigator tells you: where you are; where you should aim for and; how to get where you want to go. A navigator will have the tools to determine these things. For example, to decipher where a company is at the moment, you may need information from existing data sources on sales, profits, costs, type of product sold, exceptions to budget. In addition, a good navigator will know which of these data sources means more than others, which is more reliable, and so on. They will want to know, in order to locate 'where you are', information about competitors, suppliers and customers. They can then assess their relative position rather than an absolute one. The latter will tell them if they can meet budget, please the shareholders with their price ratios, or are going bankrupt. The former will let them know something about a long term competitive position as well as which kinds of products or offerings please customers more.

DIRECTION, MOVEMENT AND SPACE

The task of the navigator is also to know which direction to go in and take the organisation there. The roadmap for organisations is entirely unclear. It is hard to know where one is, let alone where to head. Unlike real-life navigation, where you have a map to follow, already provided, with an organisation it means traveling through uncharted terrain without a map. Even if you see a competitor in that area, it need not mean you take your organisation on a similar course. You can learn from a competitor only if you can take the piece of information about them, their 'bearings' and know whether or not to use that for your organisation at that time.

A navigator knows who to listen to and they can travel across uncharted territory without a qualm. What matters is the terrain ahead, and where to aim for.

The main three-dimensions for the Navigator are: Movement, Direction and Space.

He or she is the one concerned with the direction and route of the company. Not just with what the company is doing. Because of the role they play Navigators are often consultants, hired hands. They give prompts and, occasionally, have a few bright ideas which change everyone's direction. They generally see the priorities quite quickly. The nature of their prompts is usually positive and these people, the navigators, tend to be so in general anyway. People who play this role are quite distinctive.

WALKING AT THE SAME TIME

The best navigators are those who can use a 'compass', set a future course and *walk at the same time*. It is necessary for a navigator to set a course while walking and moving rather than standing still. This brings in another dimension of reality – that you are in constant motion whilst making decisions and taking actions. The navigator is very different than a person who sets very clear objectives and reaches them. The clear objectives may impress but may be irrelevant to the business achieving its real purpose or direction. They may be just good objectives.

A good Navigator, on the other hand, knows what the leading indicators are, or has learnt what they are. They are oriented to what moves the organisation; and what moves it forward.

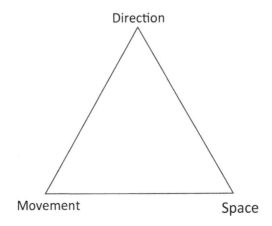

Figure 6.1   Movement, direction and space

NAVIGATOR

- Can use a 'compass'
- Knows the direction the organisation should go in
- Creates movement
- Acts while in motion
- Knows what the leading indicators are
- Can take an independent view
- Can skimp on money and resources

CHARTING A NEW BANK

I once worked as an OD consultant for a large company in Holborn, London, one of the most reputable in the City. Its Chief Executive of the time set in train a series of organisational changes aimed at creating a long term direction and aims of the company as well as its constituent parts. Partly from visiting other countries across the globe, they determined that what was needed for the company was a bank. Their primary business was insurance and financial instruments, and a bank seemed a highly credible addition. There was a fair amount of debate since this seeming skunkworks would be run by an external recruit, an MD, one used to building growth with few staff, acting at a far more rapid pace than its parent. They were in the midst of discussions about this strategy when the Chief Executive was dismissed, over questions of impropriety. However, the new MD continued with the strategy of a standalone bank alongside the corporation. The strategy people, my clients along with the corporate HR group, were called to help build the new company and were involved in choosing the new MD. He was a Navigator. Only that role could satisfy the initial requirements on him. He had uncharted territory and no previous expertise he could draw on to advise him. He had to do it by the seat of his pants. What would you learn/do differently if you acted in this role?

THE MODEL OF CHANGE: THE NAVIGATOR

In one large UK company, one Division that held with what a business partner and I were doing as consultants, no matter what, was the Customer Services division. They had massive tasks to perform and were always interested in what we had to say at a conceptual level as well as suggestions for action in their division. The MD and his team wrestled like fury with making their division perform better and meet budget.

One of the discussions we had mirrored what I have come now to call a difference between ageing and changing. The MD and his troops were trying to beat the pressures in their division that made them simply age (which can masquerade as change) rather than really change.

Change does not occur just because something in the organisation is different. The latter, being simply different, can occur just because the organisation has aged. Managers are always active and things happen and get done when they are around. Sometimes this has nothing to do with the real agenda of change, even though it may appear to be so. For example in the division I have just referred to, many actions were set out in goal form in strategies to action change. If you are not careful, you will have defined a set of actions, all dutifully carried out, but they merely represent what the organisation is likely to have done anyway. The latter process is ageing even if the actions appear under a banner of change.

Figure 6.2 illustrates the difference between ageing and change. Change occurs when the organisation is substantively different after one year. Scoping this out is Navigator territory. The measure of getting older over 1 year is OA. The measure of real change is AB. This measure can only occur in one years time (hence I have called it time=n+1 where n equals the time in the current year). You do not measure change as something that occurs from now to 1 year because the only real measure of it is the difference between where you are in 1 year after ageing one year and the actual position, also in year 1, of substantive change. When AC occurs the organisation is going backwards (in terms of substantive change).

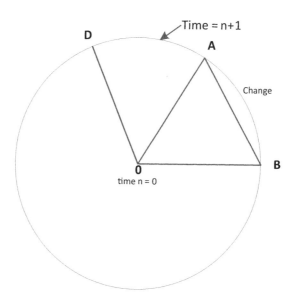

Figure 6.2   Ageing versus change

In other words change occurs in the future 'space'. To create change you need the Navigator to navigate space and time.

Navigators carry maps like this in their heads. They are visual and spatial. Navigators as OD consultants are often drawing maps demonstrating where the organisation is and where it should be. They are busy setting a course and reaching a destination whilst doing other things.

GETTING ANOTHER PERSPECTIVE: MOTIVATION OF KNOWLEDGE WORKERS

Navigators can get a fix on their position by using any kind of 'compass'. I use many and then choose what is appropriate at the time. For example, I use Jung (see Appendix 2), many psychological indicators, as well as many pieces of research. The one that I have chosen for this chapter is very simple and gives us a navigational fix on knowledge workers and on motivation. I use this one often precisely because we assume that knowledge workers are motivated by the same thing as everyone else, yet this research establishes that they are not (Garden, 1997). In most companies there is usually a clear recognition that employees are their greatest asset. There is a much less clear view of what exactly it is that motivates their people. This is particularly so with knowledge workers.

The motivation profile was obtained by asking one forced choice question asking respondents to make trade-offs between six categories or 'reasons for working' interpreted as motivational goals. This model was an interpretation from that of Professor John Hunt of London Business School's Organisation Behaviour Department (Hunt, 1986) and sanctioned by him. The six reasons are:

a) Money and a comfortable lifestyle
b) Recognition for competence and achievement
c) Structure and security
d) Working with people who are friends
e) Power influence and responsibility for others
f) Autonomy and creativity.

Each category must be traded off against the other five, obtaining a measure of relative, not absolute, importance of each category.

There were three primary factors as reasons for working in the high tech sample. The first was money and a comfortable lifestyle; the second being recognition and the third autonomy. What was not wanted by these high tech employees was structure and security, power and influence over others nor friendships.

The most important facet was that theirs was *quite unlike* the profiles obtained for any other employee. The combination of money with recognition and autonomy is what makes this profile unique. Those who have a technical orientation as well as those who are considered achievers in organisations sacrifice the first three reasons for the last three. In other words, when forced to choose, they place less importance on money and not on power. Employees who place a relatively high importance on money also tend to favour security and friendships and trade these for the latter three categories. Such a latter profile is typically found in clerical or process workers.

Interviews suggested that the priority given to money and comfort in the knowledge workers is not reflecting an attitude of money at all costs but an expectation of money being used for the purposes of autonomy. This combination, for example, allows the employee considerable mobility. Also, attaining a comfortable level of income was extremely important so that they were not burdened or hassled by the mundane demands of the world.

As such, this research acts as a map and compass for a Navigator. I call this kind of research a 'compass' because it enables you to get your bearings. With this, I have a compass fix on the present space, an idea of where to try to get to and the momentum to get there.

OD TOOLS TO LEAVE WITH NAVIGATORS

Books: Jung, C.G. 1971; Beckhard, D. and Pritchard, W. 1992; Senge P, 2006; Hunt, J. 1986; Garden, A. 1997.

Peter Senge: OD tools for Navigators

Peter Senge, one of the OD gurus of a new era, is another resource for Navigators. In The Fifth Discipline, he started with the context of the learning organisation. One of his arguments is the importance of developing reflection and inquiry for this learning organisation to occur, by promoting dialogue and avenues of inquiry. A basic idea of the book is that as "the world becomes more complex and dynamic, work must become more 'learningful'. It is no longer sufficient for one person learning for the organization … It's just not possible any longer to figure it out from the top, and have everyone else following the orders of the 'grand strategist'. The organizations that truly excel in the future will be the organizations that discover how to tap people's commitment and capacity to learn at all levels in the organization" (Senge, 2006, p. 4).

His five disciplines are as follows:

- Systems thinking
- Personal mastery
- Mental models
- Building shared vision
- Team learning starts with dialogue

The primary discipline is systems thinking, which 'contains' the other four. Systems thinking focuses on the way, and the fact, that an individual links with other components of a system. Events are "distant in time and space and yet they are all connected in the same pattern … .Business and other human endeavours are also systems. They too are bound by invisible fabrics of interrelated actions, which often take years to play out their effects on each other" (Senge, 2006, p. 6).

Senge's influence on OD is huge. The five disciplines could be mastered one by one, but that wouldn't make much sense, or be true to the overarching argument Senge builds up.

Dick Beckhard: Commitment charts

In spite of the fact that Dick, in his autobiography, several times calls himself a Catalyst (which he is) he is also a Navigator. Many of his tools are Navigators tools. Two obvious examples are his Commitment Chart and his Responsibility Charting (Beckhard and Pritchard, 1992, p. 57) each of which is referred to by Dick as a 'compass'.

A commitment chart, for example, is one of the most useful OD tools. It is used when thinking about creating a critical mass during change. This is defined as "the smallest number of people and/or group who must be committed to a change for it to occur" (Beckhard and Pritchard, 1992, p. 77). The goal is not to achieve the maximum commitment from everyone, but the minimum for the results to be as you want. During this exercise, it is apparent who is committed to which degree. So, it is partly confronting. However, it also lays out a map for the journey, which make is a Navigator's tool. People participating in the exercise can choose between these levels of commitment:

- Make it happen: These are the people who put their shoulder to the wheel of change. Not everyone has to be in this position although it can occur that people say they are in this level of commitment but are not.
- Help it happen: These are the people who have to put resources or time behind the change effort.
- Let it happen: These are the people whose commitment needs to only be a positive attitude towards the change.

- Not committed: These are the people who only need to be in neutral.
- Against: The change effort doesn't need these attitudes and actions but you can use this category to map those who are actively against the change effort.

Lewin's equation

Another good tool to get your bearings is Kurt Lewin's behavioural equation. This is expressed as: $B=f(E \times P)$. In other words, behaviour is a function of the environment and personality. This is an equation stating that any instance of behaviour is determined both by that person's environment as well as their personality and other variables specific to that person. It is common for us to think of behaviour as being too much a results of the person (their 'fault). This compass helps us keep a more level head and include factors in the environment as an equally important explanation of behaviour.

20 QUESTIONS

Which Navigator skill are you most adept at?...

....

What are the reasons for this? Your background, schooling, experience?..............

....

Can you find your direction, literally?...

....

Can you find your direction in terms of Navigating?...

....

Do you have the equivalent of a compass to guide you at work?...........................

....

Are you always going North, East, South or West?..

....

What do these four directions (NESW) represent in practice?...............................

....

Which direction is it best for the organisation to head in?....................................

....

How could you pass on your navigating skills to others?......................................

....

Are you generally a positive person?..

....

What is the best navigating metaphor for you? Driving a car, a co-pilot on a plane, or whatever?...

....

Do you have to rely on someone else to do the Navigating?.................................

....

Do you know what the leading indicators of your organisation are? Do you use them?...

....

Do you rely too much on established sources of information to be a really good navigator?..

....

Are you able to still act while in motion?...

....

Do you really change year after year or do you simply age one year?...................

....

How do you know?...

....

Do you set lots of goals to be actioned year after year?...

....

Do you understand the difference between this and changing?..............................

....

How can you teach others this difference?...

....

EXERCISES

- **Exercise One**: Using the tale of my father at the beginning of the chapter, imagine you and your organisation are, every day, required to make daring flights across terrain that is not known precisely. You are surrounded by masses of data and information. These form the context of your organisation's journey. To keep flying to your destination, what do you actually focus on to tell you where you really are in your journey? what river? building? sea? city? tells you what you really need to watch. Use your nut.
- **Exercise Two**: Why is a navigator an important role? How does it differ from setting goals and reaching them?
- **Exercise Three**: From your experience, when have you needed to be a navigator but were not? When did you play this role when another was needed? How could you get this right in future? How would you know if this was right?
- **Exercise Four**: Are you able to navigate and re-set your course while monitoring competitors, customer, etc at the same time. Can you do these two things at once? If so, can you do three things at once? Are you able to do things while in motion
- **Exercise Five**: In relation to the circle, you need to ask yourself: (1) do you know where you would end up in one year if the organisation 'got one year older' (2) do you know where you want to end up in one year if the organisation changes rather than gets one year older (3) do you have 'measures' that tell you if you have gone in the wrong direction

Table 6.1   Rate your own skill as a Navigator

	1 Awful	2 Poor	3 Adequate	4 Good	5 Superb
Scanning					
Setting a direction					
Getting real change not ageing one year					
Changing while in motion					
Working on the fly					

Total score out of 25=

Table 6.2   Rate your colleagues or team as Navigators

	1 Awful	2 Poor	3 Adequate	4 Good	5 Superb
Scanning					
Setting a direction					
Getting real change not ageing one year					
Changing while in motion					
Working on the fly					

Total score out of 25=

Table 6.3   Get someone else to rate your skills as a Navigator

	1 Awful	2 Poor	3 Adequate	4 Good	5 Superb
Scanning					
Setting a direction					
Getting real change not ageing one year					
Changing while in motion					
Working on the fly					

Total score out of 25=

CHAPTER 7

THE TEACHER

THE BEST TEACHER

The best teacher I ever had was Professor Edgar Schein of the Organizational Studies Department, Sloan School of Management, Massachusetts Institute of Technology (MIT). Nobody has since come near him in terms of teaching ability. So, what makes a teacher so good?

Knowing what he/ she is talking about and not pretending to know more than that. Being inspiring. Mostly, it comes down to the fact that they *elevate your own brain in its functioning*. With Ed, it seemed that he had created in me a new brain that functioned from then on in my own individual way. One conversation with him and you were inspired for a week.

My favourite course of all time was one taught by Ed for PhD students aimed at 'teaching you how to think'. It was sometimes based around his then-being written book on culture. The session I remember most was one where he had asked us to go away and write down 'what culture is'. Hideous task. I went home and asked the I-Ching "what is culture?" which I never admitted I'd done. I went back to class next week with my answer based on my I-Ching deliberations and largely 'got away' with my answer.

What he had tried to do was stretch our brains not simply impart knowledge. This is the role of a good OD person, the Teacher.

Learning and Teaching

Notice that there is a very different meaning to Teaching, as I am using it, and learning as others e.g., Argyris and Schon (1974), and Senge (1999) have used it. For example,.Beckhard and Pritchard also emphasise the necessity of "operating in learning mode" (1992, p. xiii). In this chapter, however important being in a learning mode is, I am emphasizing functioning in the teaching mode. This creates our sixth OD role.

OD People are about Content as Well as Process

The Teacher's role is to provide psychological content. OD work is not solely about process. I impart knowledge or teach when I deliver teachings about various psychological assessments. I do the same in all sorts of ways teaching about change. I do the same teaching about culture, about leadership and so on.

What, however, are people doing when they 'elevate people's functioning'? Well, if all they do when teaching the Myers Briggs Type Indicator™ is to disclose an individual's profile, then they are not being a Teacher; they are imparting information. If, however, they teach them how to understand and adapt to another's type without judging that other person, then they have been a Teacher. In other words, choosing this latter route makes them a genuine Teacher; they have elevated someone's functioning.

One company where there was an elevation in functioning in managers was a company based in the UK. This was a long-standing client where the two managers who were my immediate or primary clients sought to have a constant stream of transfer of teaching from me to the other managers. This is what turned the OD role in to that of the Teacher. As a result, each year we focused on a different set of teachings and the managers' functioning improved bit by bit, on and on.

INDUSTRIAL RELATIONS

When I was at university, I was required to do a thesis for my master's degree. I was asked to do one on industrial relations and, in particular, a strike which had recently occurred. The faculty of the Economics Department knew nothing about Industrial Relations and gave me the thesis topic so they would learn more. Never mind me. It was a gruesome exercise and I hated it. I did, however, discover all sorts of things. I scouted around all the manufacturing companies who employed boilermakers to find out what made their stroppy union tick, asked managers what made the boilermakers behave as they did, found out what exactly had happened in a notorious strike. It had involved 22 men in Auckland, NZ, and ended up, once arbitration had been called in, in a complete takeover of all wage negotiations by all unions by the Government. My thesis was trying to find out why the latter had been seen as inevitable by some and the 'fault' of the stupid arbitrator by everyone else. I went to see the 'stupid' arbitrator and found out exactly why the boilermakers had been found in favour of (and, hence, got a pay raise). The logic was impeccable and virtually 'forced' the hands of the arbitrator. However, this logic had never been publicly disclosed. When the reaction of the public was apparent, he had gone into a shell. He was NOT being a 'Teacher'. The latter would have treated it as an exercise in 'education' of the public, especially, for example, journalists. This is a situation where the worthiness of an individual's actions (which they were, in my opinion) were undone by the lack of impulse to be a Teacher. He should have been lauded and instead was vilified.

ED AND THE STRIPTEASE

In one class in which I was the Teaching Assistant for Ed Schein, the men had invited a striptease along. If I remember correctly, it was one man's birthday. The reaction from the class being forced to witness this striptease was, for some of them, horror and disgust, especially from the women but also from some men including a few Arabic men, unused to such exhibitions. Ed puzzled over it, trying to make a learning lesson out of it. He was advised by the main MIT admin people and in a short time they had arranged for another exhibition at the next class, but this time of an enormous poster of a naked man. When it was unveiled in the class, many of the men were horrified in their turn. However, some of them seemed to learn their lesson, at least a bit. This was typical Ed, seeing everything as a learning lesson: witness the Teacher.

ROLE MODELLING

A Teacher has to include role modeling as part of their skills set. It is impossible for a Teacher to be taken seriously if their behaviour is too much at variance with what they speak about.

When the main UK distributer of psychological instruments was set up, I was asked to sit on the board as we aimed to gain the distribution rights from the US distributer CPP. At one of the early board meetings, we discussed what each individual could bring to the party. Each person spoke in turn, including myself, but one of the key members refrained from offering anything. I kept my mouth shut about this but decided to back off from the venture and shortly afterwards decided to resign from the board.

What is actually going on in this case? The board is new and finding its way. If one person in a startup plays their role in this way while everyone else contributes you have a no-win situation from everyone. The psychological role required is the Teacher because we were dealing with role modelling behavior. The purpose of the business was about role modelling: HOW you use psychological instruments not just selling them. The former makes the psychological role they are playing that of the Teacher.

DICK BECKHARD'S PENSEE

One of the most interesting things I saw done by real Teachers at MIT was Dick Beckhard's form of assessment. I was his Teaching Assistant for a year, which included his Practicuum: his course on OD consulting. It was in that course that he asked the students for a pensee. The reaction from the Masters students was always the same: what did he mean, what WAS a 'pensee', could I do this, could I do that. He never answered them. What he said to me was "I just want them to think; to stretch themselves". So they did exactly that. What made this Teacher behaviour was not the idea of a pensee but the fact that he never answered their questions about it.

THE TEACHER

- Transfers teaching
- Brings managers down to psychological earth
- Organisation as a human being
- Role models
- Is inspiring
- Stretches your brain
- Elevates other's functioning

BRINGING MANAGERS DOWN TO PSYCHOLOGICAL EARTH

It is the role of Teacher to lead managers toward an understanding of their organisation's psychological reality. This implies, for example, not colluding in wishful thinking about creating change. It means standing one's ground when managers deny psychological reality. The purpose of this role is to bring down to psychological earth those who exist only in business reality. It is those who are relentlessly tied to a business perspective who are the ones up in the air.

MODEL OF CHANGE: THE TEACHER

One task of the Teacher is to create a concept of the organisation that is consistent with psychological reality. This is to conceive of an organisation as a human being.

Most managers treat their organisation as if it were a thing. Something solid and inanimate. This act of unity brings the organisation alive, giving it a wholeness as well as personality and 'wishes' of its own. As a working hypothesis, this gives managers a chance to make the practice of managing change comprehensible as well as effective.

Changing yourself as a Human Being

In this context, the essence of organisational change has many comparisons to changing yourself as a human being. Most of the mistakes managers make implementing change, at least from the perspective of psychological reality, stem from treating their organisation as a thing. Yet the organisation is full of people. Using the human metaphor enables managers to easily grasp the psychological condition of the organisation, as well as constraints to action that psychological reality imposes. When changing a person, for example, it is inadvisable to think of fixing them as if you were an engineer and they were a mechanical object. When an organisation is treated like a mechanical object to which one applies spanners or lasers to create change, it reacts as if it were being forced to change.

One would rarely try and force a human being to change since we know that this doesn't work. Similarly, in an organisation, forced change tends to be superficial, temporary or mightily resisted. The real spirit and behaviour in the organisation does not seem to change. Forcing produces much noise and action but remarkably little effect.

You can't change a person; at most you can only help them change. Applied to an organisation this means that we accept the organisation as being fine as it is now. It doesn't need 'fixing'. Then it can change itself. This is no different than for human beings.

EFFECTING CHANGE WITHOUT TEARING A COMPANY TO SHREDS

One of my main clients as a consultant was a medium size company. One of my greatest achievements as a consultant was to effect change in that company without tearing it to shreds. There was no large re-structuring required (only a modest amount). There were numerous interventions of various kinds (usually workshops and straight training, a development centre, strategy workshop and so on). In the midst of these workshops were numerous meetings where the real work of change intervention took place. In those meetings I acted as a psychological interpreter explaining the reasons for people's behaviour on and on and on using the various roles explored in this book. My model was to treat the organisation as a human being. Further, it was to acknowledge the company's strengths.

To start from the position that someone is wrong or inadequate will not create change but rather resistance or helplessness. The mind-set has to be to take them as they are, oddities and neuroses included.

One of my clients was, as a 'human being', an abused child. It meant that our team of 2/3 consultants had to behave quite differently to how we would naturally behave. Once we had 'figured them out' we had to stop critiquing them and steadfastly tell them exactly what they had just done right, what their strengths were. This style of consulting threw them into confusion as they were used to being berated by consultants. They loathed consultants and we were the only ones they rehired more than once; three times on completely separate programmes, for example. The fallacy in the traditional method of berating them was that the organisation never changed from previous interventions: they kept to the strategies they thought out for themselves, berating the consultants in turn behind their backs.

Applying Theories of Human Development

The metaphor of the organisation as a human being opens things up so we can apply our knowledge of human nature, especially the contingencies of human reality. It follows that well-developed theories of adult development and personality can be applied to the organisation as a whole. This metaphor suggests that the empathy we would apply to a human being with problems can also be applied to an organisation with difficulties.

Thus, the key contribution of the Teacher is to provide a mindset and a set of conceptual tools that help managers live and work within the dynamics of psychological reality.

GETTING ANOTHER PERSPECTIVE: TRYING TO BE A TEACHER WITH THE MBTI™

One of the most important things in my life, professionally, has been the MBTI™. I first learned about it when one of the members of my study group, on an MBA at Cranfield School of Management, discovered a lecturer in the Organisational Behaviour area who had a new psychological instrument and wanted to practice on some of the MBA students. We leapt for it and all did the MBTI™. In MIT for my PhD I used the MBTI™ on my research. When I finished, I went to London Business School where, guess what, I used the MBTI™ on my research on high tech employees. By that stage, I had started to use it on people and in my OD consulting. And so on. Around this time I wrote an Article on the limitations of the MBTI™. I had come across a few in my travels.

My article, (Garden 1991) titled 'Unresolved issues with the Myers Briggs Type Indicator™', was published in the *Journal of Psychological Type*, of which I was a reviewer. It took a year of back-and-forth struggle to get the article through the reviewers. To be clear: the article, a brief summary of which follows, is designed to elevate people's functioning when they use the MBTI™. It is the article of someone trying to be a Teacher. It challenges, provokes those people who use the MBTI™ but don't know anything about its research or the fact that there is some research that has never been done with the MBTI™.

In the article were four key issues. The issues highlighted were those where there was theoretical ambiguity still existing. It started from the argument that there was a difference between Jung's theory of psychological types (Jung, 1971) and Myer's theory of MBTI™ types. (Myers and her mother, Briggs, created the MBTI™) (Myers et al 2003). The MBTI™ purports to be an operationalisation of Jung's theory of types but may not be (or so I said in my article) in several respects. Arising from this theoretical ambiguity is the fact that some of the subtle, but fundamental, aspects of the MBTI™ do not have as much rigorous support as the more general (and more easily measured) reliability and validity aspects. Most studies of the MBTI™ do not validate the critical structural assumptions of the typological theory. Finding a significant positive relationship between the sensing and intuition scale and IQ tests provides support for the notion that differences on the whole S-N scale (or increasing N) means "something". However, such a result does not address such MBTI™ assumptions as that S and N are truly dichotomous types, or that the scale measures degree of preference, not degree of development. It was the latter kind of issue that Isobel Myers herself was interested in. I could tell this by reading her first Manual, the 1962 one.

Is Everybody a Type?

One of the four issues was this: One of Jung's basic premises was that not everyone should be considered a type. He was explicit about this when writing about extraversion and introversion: He stated that, for him, not everyone was extraverted or introverted: "There is a third group, and here it is hard to say whether the motivation comes chiefly from within or without. This group is most numerous and includes the less differentiated normal man, who is considered normal either because he allows himself no excesses or because he has no need of them. The normal man is influenced as much from within as from without. He constitutes the extensive middle group" (Jung, 1971, p. 516).

Further, it is only habitual use of a function, or attitude that equates with being a type, while in MBTI™ theory it is a preference, however slight, which equates with being one type rather than another. Validation of this tenet of Myer's theory has been limited and the evidence equivocal. That is the first issue. I am not imparting information but trying to get people to think above the level they might ordinarily.

The other three issues are more complex so I have not described them.

This article, with its four issues, was taken up by the British Psychological Society to use in their exam for psychology graduates to pass in order to be able to purchase the MBTI™ from the distributor in the UK. This was presumably because the article was in the Teacher mode, in other words it challenges the reader and requires them to think and think through.

OD TOOLS TO LEAVE WITH THE TEACHER

Books: Schein, E.H. 2010; Schein, E.H. 2013; Scharmer, C.O. 2009; Garden. A. 1991; Jung. C.G. 1971.

Otto Scharmer and U Theory

Otto Scharmer's U theory is primarily a Teaching theory. In it he challenges us to a higher level of functioning to save the planet, as well as organisations and ourselves.

U theory is derived from concerns that range from the political to the personal. On the one hand, "One of the primary issues is and remains that our current global system works for only a relatively small elite minority of us … Across the board, we collectively create outcomes (and side effects) that nobody wants. Yet the key decision makers do not feel capable of redirecting this course of events in any significant way" (Scharmer, 2009, p. 2). His purpose is, therefore, to create a social technology of transformational change "that will allow leaders in all segments of society, including in our individual lives to meet their existing challenges" (Scharmer, 2009, p. 5).

In U theory, Otto Scharmer shows how people and organisations can develop a range of capacities in order to create a future that might not otherwise be possible. The seven leadership capacities are developed by going down and up a U shape.

The capacities in the U shape are as follows:

- "Downloading: structuring patterns of the past-viewing the worlds through one's habit's of thought
- Seeing: suspending judgment and seeing reality with fresh eyes-the observed system is separate from those who observe
- Sensing: connecting to the field and attending to the situation from the whole-the boundary between observer and observed collapses, the system begins to see itself
- Presencing: connecting to the deepest source, from which the field of the future begins to arise-viewing from source
- Crystallizing vision and intention-envisioning the new form the future that wants to emerge

- Prototyping living microcosms in order to explore the future by doing-enacting the new through 'being in dialogue with the universe'
- Performing and embodying the new in practices and infrastructures-embedding the new in the context of the larger co-evolving ecosystems" (Scharmer, 2009, p. 6).

One of the uses of the U is to future sense not just past sense. What Scharmer sees is "a new form of presence and power that starts to grow spontaneously through small groups and networks of people. It's a different quality of connection, a different way of being present with one another and with what wants to emerge" (Scharmer, 2009, p. 4).

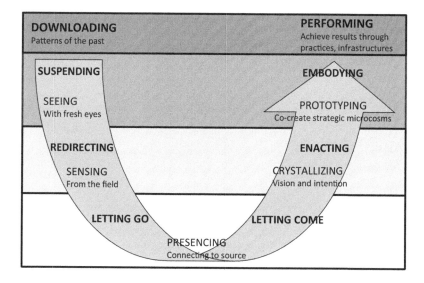

Figure 7.1   Scharmer's U theory

Source: Reprinted with permission of the publisher. From *Theory U*, leading from the future as it emerges. 2009 by C.O.Scharmer, Berrett-Koehler Publishers, Inc., San Francisco, CA.

Ed Schein: Culture

Schein elevates our functioning with all his books, most clearly in his culture books. In other words he is not simply imparting information. This can be seen even in the definition which is "a pattern of shared basic assumptions learned by a group as it solved its problems of external adaptation and internal integration which has worked well enough to be considered valid and therefore to be taught to new members as the current way to perceive, think and feel in relation to those problems" (Schein, 2010. p. 18).

David Rock

David Rock's work is a tool OD people can use. His aim is to transform people's performance at work by explaining key discoveries about the human brain. By understanding your brain, you can change the way it functions. In essence he is triyng to improve your functioning as a human being (Teacher). He is best known for his scarf model. That is status, certainty, autonomy, relatedness and fairness (SCARF). Rock states that "there are five domains of social experience that your brain treats the same as survival issues. These domains form a model" (Rock, 2009, p. 195).

20 QUESTIONS

Are you a Teacher?...

....

Do you explain 'psychological reality' to others?...

....

Can you use the metaphor of the organisation as a human being?..........................

....

Do you treat the organisation as a 'thing'?...

....

What are the organisation's ambitions? What is its past career?............................

....

How many Teachers are there around you?..

....

When have you been aware of having your functioning elevated?.........................

....

What were the consequences of that for you?..

....

Do others thank you for having spoken to them?...

....

When was the last time you had a conversation that lifted you up in functioning?...

....

When was the last time you lifted someone else up in terms of functioning?.........

....

Do people acknowledge you as a Teacher?...

....

Do you act as a role-model for what you teach? Is what you do parallel to what you say?..

....

Do you have other role models around you?..

....

Are you aware when your functioning has improved or are you oblivious to it? ..

....

Do you consciously take on a teaching role or do you avoid it?............................

....

Can you extract elevated functioning from odd episodes in your life.....................

....

Do you focus on who needs to learn or who needs to teach?................................

....

Do you stop what you are doing in the organisation to teach someone?................

....

When have you seriously challenged someone in order to teach something...........

....

EXERCISES

- **Exercise One**: The essence of this exercise is to work out who you can be a Teacher to (in the true sense of elevating their functioning) and who can be a Teacher to you (also in the sense of elevating your functioning). Now talk to them.
- **Exercise Two**: Write down all the things you morally believe strongly. Imagine you are supposed to be a role model in those things: which of those beliefs are you acting out as a role model and which are you not.
- **Exercise Three**: Write down an image/metaphor for your organisation-as-human-being. Imagine it, in the whole, IS a human being. What kind of human being is it? Use your imagination. Is it young/old; a child, teenager, adult, old person? What is its character and personality? if you were to describe your organisation-as-a-human being to a friend, what would you say about it? What is happening to your organisation at the moment and how does this organisation respond?
- **Exercise Four:** Are you wise or clever? One of the attributes of a Teacher is wisdom. Draw a line down the middle of a page of paper. Down the left hand side write all the ways in which you are wise and one the right hand side write all the ways you are clever. Which list is longer?
- **Exercise Five**: What is happening at the moment in terms of organisational change? Where is it stuck/why/what can be done about this? Why is it resisting this change? How could you talk to it to encourage it to get over that resistance?

SKILLS RATING

Table 7.1   Rate your own skill as a Teacher

	1 Awful	2 Poor	3 Adequate	4 Good	5 Superb
Bring managers down to psychological earth					
Are you a role model					
Elevate other's functioning					
Get others to think					
Open to other's ideas					

Total score out of 25=

Table 7.2   Rate your colleagues or team as Teachers

	1 Awful	2 Poor	3 Adequate	4 Good	5 Superb
Bring managers down to psychological earth					
Are you a role model					
Elevate other's functioning					
Get others to think					
Open to other's ideas					

Total score out of 25=

Table 7.3   Get someone else to rate your skills as a Teacher

	1 Awful	2 Poor	3 Adequate	4 Good	5 Superb
Bring managers down to psychological earth					
Are you a role model					
Elevate other's functioning					
Get others to think					
Open to other's ideas					

Total score out of 25=

CHAPTER 8

THE GUARDIAN

BEING ETHICAL

There are a number of implications that follow from the six previous roles. Together these create a final role for the OD person, that of the Guardian. This is one of the dominant roles I play as an OD consultant. At base, this role ensures that action within psychological reality is *ethical and not simply effective.*

STOPPING SCAPEGOATING

One of the consulting activities I have performed is an OD consultant to Unilever's fast track graduates in the UK. Every year I was hired to teach them for a day and a half and instill in them an understanding of people and teams. There were five teams in all each time. They had been in that team for four days before I saw them. It made sense, therefore, to use their experience in their teams to self-evaluate. The graduates used to love this session. I introduced a psychometric test but, for the most part, they did intensive navel-gazing on what they had been like as a team member, and as a team.

Once, however, I walked into one debriefing and smelled a rat. Something was going wrong with this team, something was up. It wasn't immediately clear what it was, so I stayed with this team and listened. It soon emerged that we had a scapegoating session going on. One member of the team was being ganged up on. The team was evaluating their behaviour over the four days but was blaming one person for most of what went wrong for the team. I was furious. I read it as scapegoating because of the dynamic in the energy in the group; the pleasure the others got from their blaming, for example, as well as the evident collusion amongst the four doing this. It simply wasn't a normal feedback session where one person was being criticized before the others. I asked the scapegoat how he was feeling, and he was clearly angry and, I suspected, a little scared. I asked them what was going on in the group; how they had got on during the week ... and so on. They responded with allegations of wrongness by the person I saw as a scapegoat who sat there not speaking. I encouraged him to respond to what they were saying. I sat in the room and kept them talking. This is the role of the Guardian.

INCORPORATING GOOD AND BAD

Was this about teaching them Effectiveness of the organisation. Only partially. Was it about Efficiency? No. It was about values and self-discipline, self-awareness. It was about good and bad. Very few organisations teach about good and bad interpersonal situations. They assume that good and bad are taken care of and also assume that their organisation is good except for rare exceptions. Alternatively, they have a culture which is dog eat dog so they don't care much about good and bad.

Both Ed Schein, who talked about the "sacredness of a human being" in his teaching and writing (Schein, 1999, p. 109), and Dick Beckhard, who defined the "health of an organization" in his original definition of OD, (Beckhard, 1969) were oriented to the ethics and sanity of organisational life. Ed states (PC, p. 174) "the process consultant cannot evade [these difficult judgements] if he defines the overall health of the organization as his basic target". The review book of OD written by Joan Gallos noted that the "power of OD's legacy and contributions is in the fields enduring respect for the human side of enterprise" (Gallos, 2006, p. xxiii).

Andmapping

Valuation of good and bad occasionally overlaps with effectiveness. Good and bad means that the right person is promoted; that the right person is seen as a high performer. These are ethical issues as much as effectiveness issues. Usually, in my opinion, they are not done correctly. A company I have worked with on competencies has a first class system of determining who are the real high performers using a system called Andmapping. One of their common findings is that the people who have a lot of self-confidence are not the high performers. Those ones who 'step' up to new situations are the ones with lots of self-confidence but without the commensurate real performance. Those who are the real high performers are quite humble. To a Guardian, this is an issue of good and bad not simply effectiveness. It is a moral issue partly because of the effects on others of the wrong person being promoted.

WHAT DOES THE GUARDIAN ACTUALLY DO?

The Guardian role relates more to what they KNOW rather than what they do. They know about goodness and badness; about the importance of valuation not just efficiency; that an organisation's natural state is healthy not unhealthy; that a major dynamic is polarization around different emotional states; that there is a collective dynamic in organisations which individuals act out

Table 8.1   What the Guardian does is to know:

Non-Guardian role	Guardian role
Only effectiveness	Goodness and badness
Efficiency	Valuation not just efficiency
Need to fix unhealthy state	Natural state is healthy
Emotions run riot	Depolarisation around emotional states
Individuals blamed	Acting out collective emotions
Unnecessary chaos	Place of sanity

The guardian is a role that preserves and protects. There is often a person in organisations who speaks words to create sanity and a place of safety. The individuals behind these words are the Guardians of the organisation, the ones who, irrespective of job title or role, protect and keep the organisation alive and on an even keel. A Guardian pays attention to things like this: that joint undertakings go well, that in emergencies extra effort is put forth.

Making People Redundant

Another time I played the dominant role of the Guardian was when a client started making people redundant with the intention of making the company more efficient. I was normally within reach by phone of the employees and I started getting stressed phone calls from them taking up most of my day. I started getting very tired but, for the most part, I continued taking these calls. After a while I decided charging the company for these calls; something I hadn't done before. The paymasters didn't like it. I continued anyway, partly because the level of distress for some people was great. This was because of the way these changes were being made and also because of the awful behaviour of the consulting company they had hired to do this job. It cost me money and certainly energy. In the end I left the company because the effect on my energy was catastrophic. Up until then I had been a Guardian!

THE CONCEPT OF VALUATION

Another way of thinking about situations that the Guardian will get involved in is with philosophy. The concept of 'valuation' describes the process of valuing in terms of, say, pleasant or unpleasant. Or, in terms of goodness and badness. Do you evaluate things in terms of their real valuation, what value they have in terms of goodness (not badness), of virtue?

Faith, Hope and Charity

The idea of effectiveness in organisations could, for example, include the three virtues of Faith, Hope and Charity.

Table 8.2　Faith, hope and charity

Faith	Hope	Charity
Have faith the organisation will do 'the right thing'	Have hope that the organisation will make it	Have generosity as a core value
Have faith the people will act with goodness not badness	Have hope that people will fulfil their potential	Have compassion in the organisation
Have faith in the ability of senior management	Have hope that goodness will prevail	Have patience with peoples effectiveness
Have faith in the organisation's future	Have hope in the organisation's future	Have a charitable approach to the organisation's future

WHAT DOES IT MEAN TO PLAY THE GUARDIAN ROLE IN AN ORGANISATION?

To perform this role, a Guardian must assume that an organisation, in its natural state, is healthy not unhealthy. Secondly, they must assume that an organisation's basic intent is to become healthier. This goes beyond the idea of helping it become more successful to helping it become healthier. If there is a natural thrust to change inside psychological reality it is that interventions should be directed towards the organisation recovering a naturally healthy state not fixing an unhealthy state (see Chapter 4: The Cultivator).

Table 8.3　Good versus effective organisations

	Effective	Ineffective
Good	Healthy	Loser
Bad	Dangerous	Deformed

Refusing a New Product

My favourite client was a fund management company in the City of London. One of the reasons it was my favourite is demonstrated by the following. The executive committee had had a discussion about a new product idea. It would have made a profit for the company but the executive committee wouldn't go ahead with it. This was because the product wouldn't have been good for the customer, although it would have been 'good' financially. This event was repeatedly told around the company, to the great delight of the employees. The company had chosen the path of goodness not just effectiveness or efficiency. What is interesting is that, while they operated like that (their operating model INCLUDED good over bad) they were very successful in terms of financial measures.

A summary of attributes of the Guardian is:

THE GUARDIAN

- Concerned with good and bad
- Protects scapegoats
- Acts from faith hope and charity
- Stands up for things
- Examines themselves
- Assumes organisation is healthy not unhealthy
- Awake to the collective phenomena

REFUSING THE CONTRACT

Another insight into the Guardian role came with a large manufacturing company in the UK. Here, for the one and only time in my career, I did a presentation to try to win a contract. I loathed doing it and loathed the reaction even more. I was hassled with difficult questions. The three man grilling committee were obtuse and, in my opinion, out-of-it as far as human resources were concerned. I went away aware only of the fact that there was something wrong with this company. I let them know I was not up for the contract; didn't want it. It was worth quite a bit of money but I didn't, as I told them, want to work for a company where, to work for them, you had to render people dysfunctional, deformed, to get to the top. This is another no-brainer. There was no inner conflict about foregoing money to avoid doing 'bad'. The company was a bad company. I learned soon after from talking with Charles Hampden-Turner that he had that company on his hit list and would never work for them. He told me that other consultants had them on a black list because they were so "revolting". I took it as an initiate rite as a consultant. Later, when I was hiring consultants, I would only hire those who had at some stage refused to do a contract, as an initiation rite. In other words, they are less likely to be bought.

MANAGING YOURSELF

To decipher whether or not an organisation is good or bad you need to decipher yourself and your own reactions. Many OD people have some means of understanding themselves. Mine are Jungian theory (refer Appendix 2), and, to a lesser extent the Myers Briggs Type Indicator™, Gestalt, Assagioli, Will Schutz especially his original Firo measures and the Elements, Ian Gordon Brown as well as a spiritual disciplines.

Ed Schein in his early version of Process Consulting wrote that, in relation to process consulting, "more important than the focus of [interpersonal and group events], however, are the attitude and philosophy that underlie the [OD] consultant's behavior vis-à-vis the client" (Schein, 1988, p. 3).

Understanding yourself is THE most important attribute and discipline of an OD person. It means understanding yourself as an instrument or tool to do your OD work (whatever roles you are). (Gestalt 1974, p. 18)

WARREN BENNIS: THE IMPORTANCE OF THE SELF

Probably the clearest voice voicing the idea that leaders need to be conscious of their self, should be authentic, i.e., author of one's creation, yourself, is Warren Bennis. In his book, On Becoming a Leader (2009, p. xxv) he draws out "four essential qualities" that are in addition to the qualities described in the book. These four are "First, they are able to engage with others by creating shared meaning ... Second, all authentic leaders have a distinctive voice ... [by which he means] a purpose, self-confidence and a sense of self ... the third quality that all true leaders have is integrity ... One component of integrity is a strong moral compass. It need not be religious faith, but it is a powerful belief in something outside one's self ... the key competence [the fourth] is adaptive capacity" . Notice that much of this is covered in what I have described in the Guardian role; a sense of self, integrity, being authentic, a sense of something outside oneself.

"I am surer now than ever that the process of becoming a leader is the same process that makes a person a healthy, fully integrated human being ... Timeless leadership is always about character, and it is always about authenticity (2009, p. xxviii).

TAKING YOUR RESPONSIBILITIES SERIOUSLY

Often you are a Guardian vis-à-vis other consultants. I can remember one time at London Business School where I had been hired to work with BP Oil Exploration. This was some time ago. The mid-senior managers had been sent on this very expensive course so that they would be more strategic in their thinking and would take more responsibility. I was day 4 and 5 of a 5 day course. I arrived to a sea of about 20 male faces (there were hardly any women). I asked them what they had learned so far. They replied, en masse, that they had learned about strategic concepts. I asked what they had learned about them. They said that wasn't up to them it was up to their senior managers. I did a double take, absolutely flabbergasted since I knew the objectives of the programme. They had learned the reverse of what they were supposed to. I did some facilitation instead of teaching. I sent them all off to their syndicate rooms to work out what they had learned for themselves. I didn't comment on what these consultants (all famous) had done before me so it was all a bit tricky. It was a tough one and a half days as they had become totally dependent and wanted to sit back and not take responsibility for running the company. My response was that of the Guardian. (Trying to do for the client what they were paying for). What mattered was that the consultants had not taken full responsibility for doing what the organisation wanted. They satisfied their own predilections rather than get out of their own comfort zone (teaching strategy).

THE MODEL OF CHANGE FOR A GUARDIAN

In the chapter of the Translator, I talked of the idea that, when working with resistance, I always assume there is positive intent behind any resistance. The Guardian is, instead, focused on the 'charge' that exists in the organisation during change: the emotional charge of both people resisting and those driving the change. Many times it is the energy around the situation rather than the reality itself that is being fought over.

In a change situation, many people start acting out one of the emotions set out in Figure 8.1. However, each emotion is polarized. Withdrawal sets off Hysteria and vice versa. Aggression sets off Passivity. Passivity sets off Aggression. What is the Guardian's role in this? To diffuse the 'energy' and get to the bottom of the issue. To focus people's reaction on being a reaction to something of substance not a reaction to another dysfunctional (but understandable) emotional state.

Emotional Charge

Organisations are full of emotional and unconscious charge. The existence of such charge can be seen everywhere as an organisation begins moving toward real rather than ephemeral change. One issue here is that, even where the intent to change is widely held, the organisation itself may not want to change AS WELL AS want to change. The task of a Guardian is encouraging managers to work with this fact not against it.

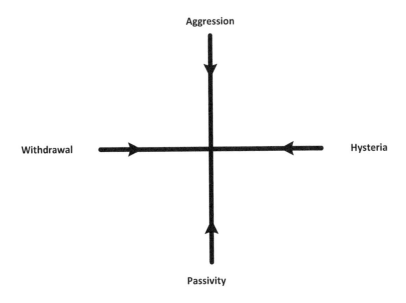

Figure 8.1   Polarisation during change

Being Used by the Collective

The Guardian must be prepared to understand how individuals can be 'used' by an organisation's collective psychology. Inside psychological reality individual human beings channel or speak the voice of the organisation's collective psyche. Different parts of the organisation act out the tensions and differences present in the organisation. For example, some parts of the organisation may take up the role of the resistor during change. This resistance will be acted out and spoken by people acting as lightning conductors for the rest. In a sense they are acted through – and more charged with- emotion than merely their own. Burke, 2006, "stated "Bion, for example, believed … that there is a … group unconscious – a collective unconscious that is more than the sum of individual unconsciousness" (p. 45).

The role of resistor, for example, is easily personalized. If the particular individual who's channelling the organisation's resistant voice is removed or side-lined, within a short time someone else may start to express this voice.

Enthusiasts on the side of change also can become filled up with an additional boost of emotional energy and become more charismatic, more positive or arrogant. It is these collective boosts of energy that can make the dynamic of change so charged. The task of the psychological interpreter at such times is mediating the different voices of the organisation, showing them to be collective rather than personal.

Knowing what is happening without being caught up in it can create objectivity and a place of sanity. This, in fact, can be the major contribution of the Guardian during a time of real change.

GETTING ANOTHER PERSPECTIVE: USING YOURSELF AS AN INSTRUMENT

An OD tool I use a great deal was mentioned in Chapter 2, the Seer. It fits also with the emphasis in this chapter on managing yourself and using yourself as an instrument. Schutz's Elements vary from those that examine the level of Behaviour, as well as Feelings and Self-concept. (Schutz, 1984).

Every key OD person in my life has accentuated the notion that you monitor yourself as part of your OD work. Table 8.4 below gives you an idea of how to use Schutz's three dimensions to find out more than you knew.

Table 8.4   Data about your feelings that you can use for diagnosis

Schutz' dimension	Unhealthy	Healthy
Inclusion/ Significance	You get bored, you get hyped-up; you can't pay attention, you feel excluded or overly included	You are easily able to pay attention; you have a clear role and identity; you stay awake
Control/ Competence	You keep dropping things; you are uncoordinated physically; you are tense and worrying	You stay on top of things; you are physically coordinated; you like to compete a little
Openness/Likeability	You don't like the people around you; you feel distant from people or overly close; you don't care	You generally like people; you care about what you are doing; you like yourself; you trust others

Source: Adapted from FIRO theory by Dr. Will Schutz. Used with permission of Business Consultants, Inc.

If your feelings relate to the inclusion area, for example, you can diagnose that this is the area in the organisation that is 'active', or needs attention. This is to use yourself as an instrument or tool.

A related but equally basic stance is to see that what you are experiencing from the organisation will have its counterpart in you. If you are being shut out in the organisation, some part of you will be shutting another part of you out. This is where disciplines such as sub-personalities (below) or the Jungian functions are invaluable.

OD TOOLS TO LEAVE WITH GUARDIANS

Ian Gordon-Brown: Centre for Transpersonal Psychology

The Centre for Transpersonal Psychology was created by Ian Gordon-Brown and Barbara Somers in London many years ago. They used to run numerous workshops on various aspects of the transpersonal. Up to a certain date I went on every workshop two-three times. For some of them I was walked through each workshop in one-to-one sessions with Ian. They remain one of the most important formative influences on my life.

Transpersonal psychology is an umbrella term referring to several approaches which integrate ancient knowledge and modern knowledge. In other words, some of the old mystery schools, a lot of Jung, Psychosynthesis, Symbolism, Archetypal psychology such as that written about by James Hillman, were all brought into the Centre for Transpersonal Psychology to bring to life a tremendous psychological mix. In particular, this psychology emphasizes the collective and how you can get caught up in it or access it (part of the Guardian's territory). Symbolically, their model of the psyche as it was seen is illustrated in Figure 8.2.

"This map shows onion-like rings in the dynamic of the personality. The conscious ego emerges upward from behind a mask, holds the unconscious at bay and begins to integrate the more consciously-functioning aspects of the psyche … These images are seen by us, not imposed from outside … Talking with them, befriending them, we can led back closer to our own basic purpose". (p. 15)

- The persona is concerned with roles and masks. They accommodate how the inner person likes to appear outwardly.
- The ego is incarnated from the Self. It is shown in the world. Behind the persona and its masks is the person who wears the masks (the ego).
- The shadow is the part of ourselves that is pushed down and to the back, not immediately acceptable. "Gradually, we come to realize that this is really our projection of our Self" (Gordon-Brown, 2008, p. 16).
- The masculine and feminine originate from our contact with our parents. Both are experienced by any one individual.
- Archetypal levels. This is the collective layer which relates to the archetype of the Self as well as other collective energies.

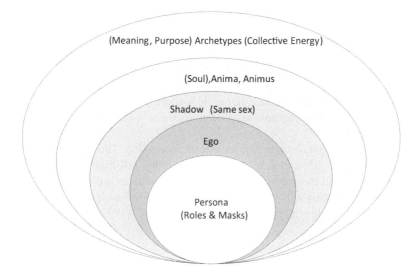

Figure 8.2   Onion map from Ian Gordon-Brown
Source: This figure is reproduced from The Raincloud of Knowable Things by Ian Gordon-Brown with Barbara Somers with permission from Archive Publishing, Blandford Forum, Dorset, UK.

The word, 'transpersonal' assumes that our ego and the psyche are in a much larger container than most in the West would normally assume. Like psychosynthesis and Jung, they believe that we hunger after something higher, have a Higher Self, and a spiritual consciousness. This higher self can be accessed by delving deep in our psyche and thereby start to reach our potential. The word 'Transpersonal' implies that people are looking beyond the personal. As Ian says: "Transpersonal psychology is about consciousness. It looks towards oneness, cosmic awareness and meta-needs, aiming towards essence, being rather than doing … It is concerned with transcendence of the ego-self, with ultimate meaning and self-transcendence". (Gordon-Brown, 2008, p. xxv)

Warner Burke: A Normative View of OD

The shift is generally "toward a more humanistic treatment of members of all levels in the organisation" (Burke, W. 1992, p. 196).

The values he chooses to assess an organisation from a normative view of organisations include, for example:

- "Growth and development of organization members is just as important as making a profit or meeting the budget …

- Equal opportunity and fairness for people in the organization is commonplace; it is the rule rather than the exception…
- Cooperative behaviour is rewarded more frequently than competitive behaviour etc. … " (Burke, 1993, p. 197)

You can compare Warner Burke's list with Richard Beckhard's (Beckhard, 1997, p. 165). Both show a strong normative leaning.

- "Thriving organizations will have team leadership. The unique tasks of the top leaders will be to make the team leadership effective
- … More and more company policies and practices will be values-driven. Economic goals will still have to be met, but for the organisation to stay at the leading edge, attention to values is required" (1997, pp. 165–166)

Servant Leadership

Last but not least, we end with reference to Servant leadership. This is a 'management' philosophy aimed at all people. It is described by the founder, Robert Greenleaf as follows: "The servant-leader is servant first. It begins with the natural feeling that one wants to serve, to serve first. Then conscious choice brings one to aspire to lead. The difference manifests itself in the care taken by the servant-first to make sure that other people's priorities are being served. The best test, and difficult to administer, is: Do those served grow as persons? Do they, while being served, become healthier, wiser, freer, more autonomous, more likely themselves to become servants? And what is the effect on the least privileged in society; will they benefit or, at least, not be further deprived?" (quoted in Lewis and Noble, 2008).

20 QUESTIONS

Who are the Guardians in the organisation?...

....

How do they play their role?..

....

What are the unrecognized ways Guardians pay attention to the organisation?......

....

What virtues are present in the organisation?.......................................

....

What vices are present?..

....

Who in your organisation has the ability to look after what is good?.....................

....

When have you seen them behave in this fashion?...

....

When have you had the impact of a Guardian?......................................

....

What behaviour does it require?..

....

What response does it generate?...

....

What conditions were relevant at the time?...

....

What situations have you been in that required the Guardian?................................

....

Are you frightened around Guardian requirements or decisions?...........................

....

Do you sacrifice calls to be good for those to be effective....................................

....

Do you think it is right to promote the right person for ethical reasons?...............

....

Does your organisation promote the right person for ethical reasons?....................

....

Do you take on work you shouldn't?..

....

Have you experienced an 'initiation' rite as a consultant or manager or student?...

....

Have you experienced scapegoating (and can detect it)?.......................................

....

What did you do about it? Rescue the one being scapegoated?..............................

....

EXERCISES

- **Exercise One**: What are the manifestations of Faith Hope and Charity in your organisation/client?
- **Exercise Two**: How does your organisation/client balance effectiveness and ethics? How does this square up with promoting or not promoting the real performers?
- **Exercise Three**: When have you acted in a primarily ethical way in your organisation/client. How did it feel: good or scary? What was the result of your actions?
- **Exercise Four**: How could you act in a more 'sane' fashion in your organisation/client? Could you be the source of sanity and level-headedness in your organisation/client? What would you do to make that happen?
- **Exercise Five**: What are the core ethical issues in your organisation/client? How could you spearhead their being taken seriously and resolved?

Table 8.5   Rate your own skill as a Guardian

	1 Awful	2 Poor	3 Adequate	4 Good	5 Superb
Are you truly honest?					
Stick your neck out in the interests of what is good?					
Believe in faith hope and charity					
Can work with unconscious energy					
Act as a place of sanity to others					

Total score out of 25=

Table 8.6 Rate your colleagues or team as Guardians

	1 Awful	2 Poor	3 Adequate	4 Good	5 Superb
Are you truly honest?					
Stick your neck out in the interests of what is good?					
Believe in faith hope and charity					
Can work with unconscious energy					
Act as a place of sanity to others					

Total score out of 25=

Table 8.7 Get someone else to rate your skills as a Guardian

	1 Awful	2 Poor	3 Adequate	4 Good	5 Superb
Are you truly honest					
Stick your neck out in the interests of what is good?					
Believe in faith hope and charity					
Can work with unconscious energy					
Act as a place of sanity to others					

Total score out of 25=

QUESTIONNAIRE TO ASSESS YOU IN THE ROLES

WHICH OF THE OD ROLES DO YOU MOST RELATE TO? (RATING SCALE IS: 1=LEAST TO 7=MOST)

	Seer	Translator	Cultivator	Catalyst	Navigator	Teacher	Guardian
Feel drawn to most							
Others comment on							
Is most successful for you							
Would hate to lose							
Rely on in a tight corner							
Would pay most for							
Total score							

RANK ORDER YOUR ROLES

Position	Role
1st	
2nd	
3rd	
4th	
5th	
6th	
7th	

What do you want to do with the roles rated highest? Anything?

What do you want to do with the roles ranked lowest?

Any surprises?

MY CENTRAL OD COMPASS: JUNGIAN THEORY

The Jungian typological map describes two attitudes, extraversion and introversion, and two pairs of alternative functions, sensing or intuition, and thinking or feeling.

The Myers Briggs Type Indicator™ (MBTI™) (2003) 'types' people according to the preferred attitudes and functions, in other words, within each pair, which function or attitude is the most preferred. Thus if one is 'typed' as ESTJ, then this indicates that one's expressed preferences are extraverted, sensing, thinking, and judging rather than the less preferred aspects of introversion, intuition, feeling or perception. The verbal formulation that emerges is, however, just a shorthand for the complex interaction of all eight attitudes and functions. The Jungian theory behind the simple verbal formulation is not only more complex but also more dynamic than the static impression a type description conveys. In particular, we need to take into account the role of the unconscious and, subsequently, the theory of opposites.

In the MBTI™ the preferred or typed functions and attitudes are interpreted as being conscious, with the non-preferred functions and attitudes as being unconscious. In Jungian theory, the situation is more complicated and some qualifications to the above will be made.

THE MAP: THE JUNGIAN COMPASS

An underlying abstract guideline map of the four functions can be used to illustrate some of the dynamic processes involved. The four functions are often likened to the four points of a compass reflecting the fact that this is essentially a conceptual tool or framework providing guidance to orientation. The diagram in Figure A2.1 illustrates both the psychic structure and processes involved. The upper half of the circle is light, representing the conscious side, while the dark lower half represents the unconscious.

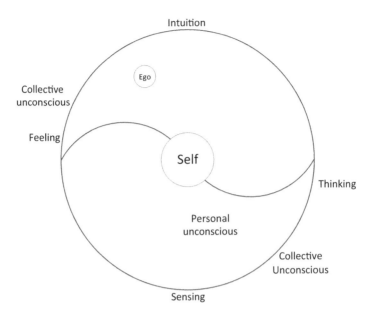

Figure A2.1   Jungian map of the psyche

Source: This figure is adapted from Ian Gordon-Brown's and Barbara Somers' workshop material observed live over many years. It does not come from published material Permission to use it in this manner has been given by Archive Publishing, Dorset, UK.

In the figure, the individual represented would be considered an intuitive thinking type (an NT on the MBTI™). Both intuition and thinking are, here, associated with the conscious sphere of the psyche. Sensing and feeling, counterparts to the two preferred functions, are shown in the unconscious sphere. Even for the individual represented in this figure, there is a further second-order preference ranking. In this instance, intuition is preferred over thinking which means the former is referred to as the 'dominant' or superior function while thinking is the auxiliary or 'helping' function. The psyche is oriented first and foremost by the intuitive function and secondly by the thinking function.

The two non-preferred functions also have, theoretically, their own second-order ranking. Since intuition is dominant the inferior function must be sensing. Since thinking is the auxiliary, its opposite function, feeling must be the tertiary or mediating function.

Development of Functions

It is considered an integral part of living that each individual will develop one function at the expense of the others, and particularly at the expense of its polar opposite. One must apply oneself to the differentiation of that function with which one is gifted or which provides the most effective means of ensuring success or survival. The developed functions and, in particular, the superior/dominant function, become the means of adapting to and experiencing the world as well as the basis around which to organise one's personality. It is usually considered that the facility of the functions is determined in some 'innate' way. Because of this, it is possible for an individual, through the presence of parents, for example, to develop most a function which is not the 'naturally' best function. This leads to the development of 'turntypes'.

How the Dynamic Happens

In spite of this qualification concerning turntypes, the more typical development is for the development of the naturally superior function. The process involved is for this function to be raised to conscious level and this emphasis inevitably means the suppression of its polar opposite, for the action of this is directly contrary to that of the dominant function. Thus, while the latter is being well developed through receiving a great deal of psychic energy, this is accompanied by a commensurate deprival of energy to the inferior function which remains in the unconscious state and as such must be diffused with and permeated by the contents of the unconscious. Since, according to Jung, all functions in the unconscious are fused together, the third and fourth functions in the previous figure would not be as separate from each other as the two conscious functions would be.

The Ego and the Direction of the Conscious Functions

Only the conscious functions are capable of direction and subject to the will of the ego since the ego is the centre of the conscious sphere. Since the ego is not the centre of the unconscious, the functions in the unconscious are not subject to the will of the ego and act autonomously subject to the Self.

Subsequent development of the auxiliary (and possibly the tertiary) involves a similar process of 'rising up' from the unconscious to the conscious spheres. Note that it is possible for only one function to be fully differentiated into consciousness, with the remaining three remaining unconscious. Alternatively three functions may be conscious, with only one function remaining unconscious.

In other words, the function which is most developed and the most conscious is the most refined and the most reliable. As one goes down the hierarchy to the inferior function, each mode of operating is less conscious, less subject to control or use by the ego. Each function becomes less able to work as 'efficiently' as the superior function and, particularly for the inferior function more uncomfortable when called upon to be used.

The Process of Righteous Identification

Not only does the superior function become relatively more differentiated, but the ego, as the centre of consciousness, becomes identified with its nature. Thus an intuitive will become identified with being creative, insightful, perceptive etc. A feeling type will become identified with being caring, concerned with other people, in tune with their own values etc. A thinking type will become identified with being rational and logical, and a sensing type with having their feet on the ground, being in touch with reality. One also tends to implicitly assume that this is the way one 'should' be and, moreover that others 'should' be. This is the dynamic that the unskilled practitioner of the MBTI™ will make worse.

Enantiadromia

In general the functions and attitude in the unconscious act as a counterweight. This is illustrated by the description from Jung: (Jung, 1960, p. 419).

> *The activity of consciousness is selective. Selection demands direction. But direction requires the exclusion of everything irrelevant. This is bound to make the conscious orientation one-sided. The contents that are excluded and in habited by the chosen direction (i.e., function) sink into the unconscious, where they form a counterweight to the conscious orientation.*

While the functions are termed 'opposites' they do not, in themselves, act in a contrary way to each other. The unconscious functions and attitude, because they, in their intrinsic nature, are opposite or unlike each other should represent merely complementary tendencies.

Tension will result if the inferior function is no longer simply 'not used' but is actively repressed. At this point the unconscious function becomes associated with the shadow complex. Note that calling the inferior function the 'shadow' is incorrect for the typology and the shadow complex are separate.

The contents of the conscious sphere can become so developed relative to the unconscious that the latter no longer 'balances' the former but acts in opposition to the aims of the conscious ego so that an in evitable tension is set off. This is when the process termed 'enantiadromia' is set off.

SELF AND INDIVIDUATION

One of the most significant ideas in Jung's theory of the psyche, and psychological types is the existence of the Self and the necessity of the process he called individuation. The Self is the centre of both the conscious and unconscious and stands in counterpoint to the ego (discussed earlier). It is wiser than the ego. It is expected that by midlife one is probably responding to the promptings of the Self and not just the ego. Associated with this process, of handing the reins to the Self, is the process of individuation which everyone is selected to begin. In essence it propels individuals to separate from societal norm and respond to what is appropriate from an internal reference point rather than an external reference point.

BIBLIOGRAPHY

Assagioli, R. *The Act of Will*. 1974, Penguin Books, Baltimore, MD.

Assagioli, R. *A Collection of Basic Writings*. 2012, Synthesis Center Publishing, Amherst, MA.

Assagioli, R. *Transpersonal Development*. 2007, Inner Way productions, Forres, Scotland.

Bailyn, L. *Breaking the Mold: Redesigning work for productive and satisfying lives*. 2006, Second edition. Cornell University, Ithaca, NY.

Beckhard, R. *Organization Development*. 1969, Reading, MA. Addison-Wesley Publishing Company Ltd.

Beckhard, R. and Pritchard, W. *Changing the Essence: The art of creating and leading fundamental change in organizations*. 1992, San Fransisco, CA, Jossey-Bass Publishers.

Beckhard, R. *Agent of Change: my life, my practice*. 1997. San Francisco, CA. Jossey-Bass Publishers.

Beckhard, R. in Gallos, J.V. *Organization Development*. 2006, San Francisco, CA, Jossey-Bass Publishers.

Bennis, W. *On Becoming a Leader*. 2009, Philadelphia, PA, Perseus Books Group.

Burke. W. *OD: A process of learning and changing, Second edition*. 1993, Reading, MA, Addison-Wesley.

Gallos, J.V. Editor, *Organization Development*. 2006, San Francisco, CA, Jossey-Bass Publishers.

Garden, A. *Burnout: The effect of personality*. Dissertation for PhD. 0373736. 1985, Cambridge, MA. Sloan School of Management, MIT.

Garden, A. The Purpose of Burnout: A Jungian Interpretation. In Perrewe, P.L. (ed.) 1991, vol. 6, No. 7, pp. 73–93. Handbook on Job Stress, Special Issue. *Journal of Social Behavior and Personality*.

Garden, A. Unresolved Issues with the Myers Briggs Type Indicator™. *Journal of Psychological Type*, vol. 22, 1991, pp. 3–14.

Garden, A. A Framework of the Psychological Reality of Organizations, in *OD Practitioner*, 1998, pp. 17–25.

Garden, A. *Reading the Mind of the Organisation: Connecting the strategy with the psychology of the business*. 2000, Hampshire. England, Gower Publishing Ltd.

Goffee, R. and Jones, G. *The Character of a Corporation: How your company's culture can make or break your business*. 1998, New York, New York, Collins Publishers Inc.

Hamel, G. *The Future of Management*. 2007, Boston, MA, Harvard Business School Publishing.

Jung, C.G. *The Structure and Dynamics of the Psyche, No 8 Bollingen Series Collected Works*. 1960, Princeton, NJ, Princeton University Press.

Jung C.G. *Two Essays on Analytical Psychology, No 7 Bollingen Series Collected Works*. 1966, Princeton, NJ, Princeton University Press.

Jung, C.G. *Psychological Types, No 6 Bollingen Series Collected Works*. 1971, Princeton, NJ, Princeton University Press.

Kotter, J. *The Heart of Change: Real-life stories of how people change their organizations*. 2002, Boston, MA, Harvard Business School Publishing.

Kotter, J. Leading Change: Why transformation efforts fail in Gallos, J.V. (ed.), *Organization Development*. 2006, San Francisco, CA, Jossey-Bass publishers.

Langer, E.J. *Mindfulness*. 1989, Cambridge, MA; Perseus Books Group.

Mann. D. *Gestalt Therapy*. 2010, Routledge, Hove, East Sussex, UK.

Maslach, C. *Burnout: The cost of caring*. 1982, Englewood Cliffs, NJ, Prentice-Hall.

Myers, I. McCaulley, M.H. Quenk, N.L. Hammer, A.L. *MBTI Manual: Third Edition*. 2003, Mountain View, CA, CPP.

Nevis, E.C. *Organizational Consulting. A Gestalt Approach*. 2001. Cambridge, MA. Gestalt Press

Polster, E and M. *Gestalt Therapy Integrated: Contours of theory and practice*. 1974, New York, New York, Random House, Inc.

Rock, D. *Brain at Work*. 2009. Harper Collins Publishers, New York NY.

Scharmer, C.O. *Theory U: Leading from the future as it emerges*. 2009, San Francisco, Berrett-Koehler Publishers.

Schein, E.H. *Process Consultation*. 1988, Reading, MA, Addison-Wesley.

Schein, E.H. *Process Consultation Revisited*. 1999, Englewood Cliffs, NJ, Prentice Hall.

Schein, E.H. *Organizational Culture and Leadership, Fourth Edition*. 2010, San Francisco, CA, Jossey-Bass.

Schein, E.H. *Helping: How to offer, give and receive help*. 2011, San Francisco, CA, Berrett-Koehler Publishers.

Schein, E.H. *Humble Inquiry*. 2013, San Francisco, CA, Berrett-Koehler.

Schutz, W. *The Truth Option*, 1984, Berkeley, CA, Ten Speed Press.

Senge, P. *The Fifth Discipline: The art and practice of the learning organization*. 2006, New York, NY, Doubleday.

INDEX

For Product Safety Concerns and Information please contact our EU representative GPSR@taylorandfrancis.com Taylor & Francis Verlag GmbH, Kaufingerstraße 24, 80331 München, Germany

Printed and bound by CPI Group (UK) Ltd, Croydon, CR0 4YY
01/05/2025
01858389-0007